C000286017

ALESIA 52 BC
The Victory of Roman Organisation

by Frédéric BEY

Maps by Pascal Da Silva and Antoine Poggioli
Translated from the French by Alan McKay

Histoire & Collections

To my Daughter Augustine…

CONTENTS

DE BRENNUS A JULIUS

The Romans had been at odds with the "Gauls" for a very long time indeed.
The Celts first invaded Italy across the Alps as far back as about -400 BC, with the Cenomani,
the Lingonii, the Boii and the Senonii settling down once and for all in Northern Italy.
Somewhere between 390 and 386 BC, a Senoni war-chief called Brennus managed to capture
Rome and ransom the city with his famous *Vae Victis*. The Urbs was then a city whose authority
was only relative. Nonetheless, the sack of Latium's capital, highlighted by Livy in his History
of Rome, helped to forge a centuries-old loathing between the Romans, ashamed of being forced
to capitulate to Brennus, and the Gauls, insolently proud of their triumph.

DURING THE FIRST CENTURIES OF THE ROMAN REPUBLIC'S existence, the traditional Gallo-Roman enmity and rivalry, going back to the time of the sack of Rome by Brennus, grew - an expression ill-feeling for Rome's long-drawn-out conquest of its Gallic neighbours' Cisalpine territories. In 295 BC Rome launched itself against the Celtic tribes of Northern Italy. Allied to Hannibal during the Second Punic War, the Gauls had earned a reprieve for themselves but had also aroused an irresistible longing for revenge on the part of the Roman Senate. At the end of the 190s BC, the Romans once and for all colonised the Pô Valley and had all the Gauls in Italy submit to their laws.

The next step was part of the competition between the "Great Powers" of the period. Independent Gaul was implicated in the global expansionist process of Roman might, which took place throughout the whole of the Mediterranean basin. Phoenicians, Greeks and Gauls were the successive victims of Rome's effort at achieving and increasing its worldwide domination. This expansion became evident with the conquest of Southern Gaul (Transalpine Gaul for the Romans). The region was reduced to the state of province in -121 and its capital, Narbonne, was founded in -118. While the Roman Republic was reaching its apogee, independent Gaul was reduced to the regions north of the Cévennes and the Valley of the Rhone. Its economic influence and its geographical situation – on the route of Germania's tin – undoubtedly made it a prey of the most appetising sort.

Finally more pragmatically, Gaul merely became a political pawn in the hands of the triumvirs Pompey, Crassus and Caesar after they took over control of the Republic at the end of its decline, from the 60s BC onwards. Pompey consolidated his reputation by putting down Asia and Spain, Crassus dreamed of conquering Mesopotamia. Julius Caesar, the least well-known and least experienced of the triumvirs, also needed somewhere where he could prove himself. Appointed Proconsul of Cisalpine Gaul and Illyricum after his time as consul, this ambitious scion of the Julii family was looking for a breakthrough.

Towards 390 BC the famous Brennus and his warriors looted Rome. 19th century art got hold of the story and changed it into a myth.

Preceding page.
Brennus with his part of the booty. The artist has been able to evoke the awful savagery of war in ancient times using the symbols and respecting the taboos of the times.
(Paul Joseph © RMN La Rochelle, Musée des Beaux-Arts)

Opposite.
A few moments before Brennus' famous Vae Victus.
(Lithography from the end of the 19th century, Private Collection, RR)

Rather unexpectedly it turned out to be independent Gaul which offered him the opportunity to reveal his talent at the head of his legions. The Gallic War was for him the ideal stepping stone towards power which he already found difficult to share.

It was therefore as a victim of what was at stake quite outside its control that Gaul so dramatically became part of Julius Caesar's political strategy. Moreover, the Romans did not have a very high opinion of the Gauls whom they always regarded as barbarians: *"To make a tentative summary: for almost all the Romans, the Gauls were fero-* *cious creatures, sacrilegious plunderers who had got hold of the Capitol and slaughtered the senators (for the French, it would be like the English burning Joan of Arc at the stake); we fought against them in terrible battles, we subjugated those who settled in Northern Italy but beware! They were different. For on the other side of the Alps there was a disturbing world which could be sparked off at any time, despite the fact that Rome had overrun part of it near Marseille. Gaul was a permanently potential danger"* [1]. In this context, Alesia was the final manifestation of this deep mistrust between the two peoples.

7

The Gallic Wars took place
at a moment when Independent
Gaul and the Roman Republic
were evolving quite separately.
After a few turbulent decades,
it seemed impossible
to thwart Rome's power whereas
on the other hand tribal dissension
and outside pressure were
undermining Gaul which
seemed to be declining, especially
after the incursions
by the Cimbri and the Teutones.

Opposite.
**The Republic on the eve
of Roman conquest.** (Map by Jean-Marie Mongin)

*Gallic Chieftain. This "naïve" illustration has
taken from a collection of "cut-out cardboard
soldiers" dating from the first half
of the 20th century.*
(Private Collection, RR)

Britannia

Germania
Inferior

Belgica

Germania
Superior

Gallia

Aquitania

Oceanus

Alpe

Narbonensis

Co

Sa

Tarraconesis

Lusitania

Baetica

Africa

Nun
Infe

MAURETANIA

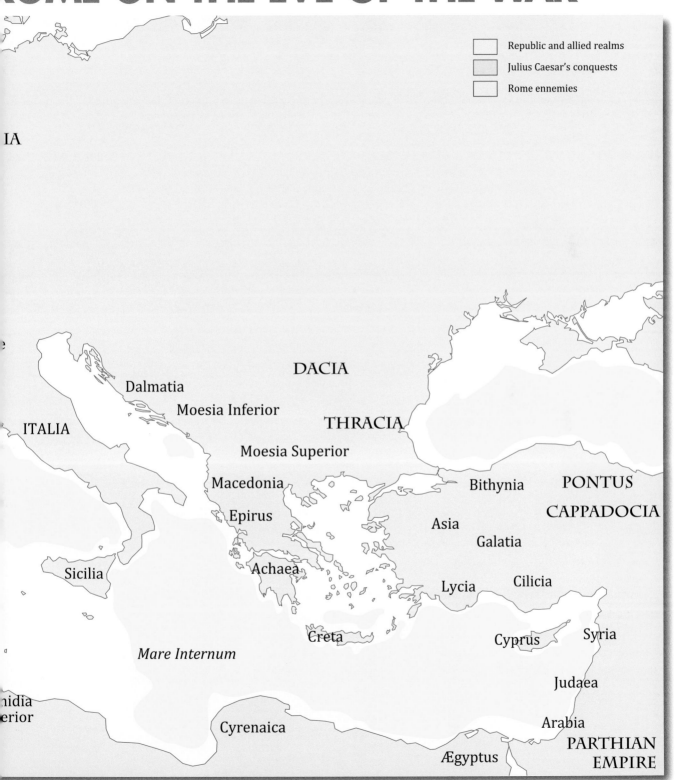

Republic and allied realms

Julius Caesar's conquests

Rome ennemies

IA

DACIA

Dalmatia

Moesia Inferior

THRACIA

ITALIA

Moesia Superior

Macedonia

Bithynia

PONTUS

CAPPADOCIA

Epirus

Asia

Galatia

Sicilia

Achaea

Lycia

Cilicia

Creta

Cyprus

Syria

Mare Internum

Judaea

nidia
erior

Arabia

Cyrenaica

PARTHIAN
EMPIRE

Ægyptus

ARRIVING FROM THE DANUBE REGION the Celts reached Gaul in several waves from the 500s BC onwards. Spreading out into Spain, Italy and the Island of Britannia (now the United Kingdom), the Gallic tribes reached the height of their power between -400 and -200.

GAUL IN 60 BC: DIVISION AND RIVALRY

Arriving from the Danube region the Celts reached Gaul in several waves from the 500s BC onwards. Spreading out into Spain, Italy and the Island of Britannia (now the United Kingdom), the Gallic tribes reached the height of their power between -400 and -200.

The sack of Rome has already been mentioned. A similar event took place at Delphos which was also the work of the Gauls. Dreaded by all their neighbours, notorious for having a voracious appetite for war, the Celts were nonetheless never able to build up anything from their various successes. The tribes were always divided politically and did nothing else but regroup into powerful rival confederations which could only fuel internecine wars. The mightier tribes sought to dominate the others, at least regionally, by tying up client tribes or by attracting them away from the influence of their adversaries. In Caesar's time, the most powerful tribes were the Aedui, the Sequani and the Arverni. For a long time the latter had been the most influential in all Gaul but had then been weakened when the Romans took their client tribes in the Rhone Valley and south of the Cévennes away from them when they conquered Southern Gaul and transformed it into a Roman province.

Their last great king, Bituit, suffered a terrible defeat at the hands of the Roman legions in 121 BC. The Roman settlements along the shore of the Mediterranean and along the valley of the Rhone marked the first stage in the deep-seated decline starting to affect the Gauls' military power. When the Cimbri and the Teutones ravaged Gaul at the head of a fairly assorted group of German and Celtic tribes in 109 BC, no generalised or organised resistance was forthcoming. Only the fierce Belgian tribes in northern Gaul managed to push back the invaders. The Cimbri and Teutones whose attacks finally reached Italy were in the end crushed by Marius and his legions. At the time, the Gauls had managed to get rid of a dangerous outside threat with the help, albeit indirectly, of the Roman armies. Subsequently the Aedui decided to win Rome's favour by countering the ambitions of their Arverni neighbours and openly became clients of the great Italian city. During Caesar's consulate no single tribe was able to impose its politics on another and from then on regional rivalries, accommodations and coalitions compromised independent Gaul's internal stability to a point which had never been reached in the past.

Using a regional classification borrowed from Jacques Harmand Gaul's political organisation in Caesar's time can be described by splitting Celtic Gaul into five sectors, using a sixth one for Aquitania and a seventh for Belgian Gaul; these last two differed because their Celtic population was less dense or because new tribes had arrived recently on their soil.

Gallia Belgica (the north of present-day France, to the north of the River Seine, and present-day Belgium) or Belgian Gaul regrouped the more recently settled tribes on the left bank of the Rhine. The great farming tribes from the south of the region, the Bellovaci, Suessiones and Rhemi, were much more civilised than the very crude and belligerent Nervii, Atrebates, Morini and Menapii. The origin of certain Belgian tribes is still uncertain with historians still hesitating between "Germanised" Celts or more or less "celtified" truly trans-Rhine Germans. Nonetheless, as a whole, the Belgian tribes differed by being more strikingly forceful militarily than their southern neigh-

Opposite.
The peoples of Gaul, on the eve of the Roman conquest.
(Map by Antoine Poggioli and Jean-Marie Mongin)

Below.
Boar hunting, forests of oaks, standing stones, the village, pig-breeding, farmers, the oppidum: all the Gauls' life has been summarised on this frieze, taken once again from the "cut-out cardboard soldiers".
(Private Collection, RR)

BRITANNIA

GERMANIA

OCEANUS

Eburones

Morini
Ménapes
Atrebates
Nervii
Atuatuci

Treveri

Unellii
Caleti
Ambiani
Veromandui
Viducasses
Bellovaques
Suessions
Baiocasses
Veliocasses
Silvanectes
Mediomatrici
Lexovii
Remi
Abrincates
Eburovices
Leuci
Esuviens
Parisii
Tribocci
Coriosolites
Meldes
Osismes
Diablintes
Carnutes
Tricasses
Lingones
Veneti
Redonse
Cénomans
Senones
Namnetes
Mandubii
Andes
Turones
Rauraci
Bituriges
Aeduni
Sequani
Pictones
Helvetii
Santones
Ambarres
Arverni
Ségusiaves
Lemovices
Allobroges
Bituriges
Petrocorii
Vellaves
Vasates
Cavares
Cadurci
Helvi
Nitiobroges
Sotiates
Gates
Gabali
Vocontii
Ruteni
Tarbelli
Elusates
Volcae
Arecomici
Sibuzati
Ausques
Volques
Salluviens
Bigerrions
Tectosages
Convènes

HISPANIA

MARE INTERNUM

bours.

Celtic Gaul, the true heartland of independent Gaul, was cut up into several regions with very varied characteristics. To the east of Belgium (present-day Lorraine, Alsace, Vosges and German Palatinate) there was a sector dominated by the powerful Treveri tribe, whose neighbouring Vangiones, Mediomatricii Nemetes or Triboces were very much influenced by the German peoples on the right bank of the Rhine. To the south of Belgium, in the sector situated to the south of the Seine, already right in the middle of Gaul, tribes like the Carnutes, Parisii or the Lingones had been settled there for a very long time together with others like the Tricassi and the Durocassi who had had to flee from the new arrivals in Belgian Gaul. The region was dominated by the Senones, at least from the demographic point of view. The most developed and most civilised area was the one situated immediately to the north of the Roman province, right in the middle of present-day France. The Arverni and their clients (Cadurci, Gabali, Vellavi), their rivals the Aedui and their clients (the Segusiavi for example), the Sequani and the Bituriges numbered among the mightiest

and wealthiest tribes in the whole of independent Gaul. To the east of this same sector, the Helvetii occupied the plateaux in present-day Switzerland. Finally two less densely populated sectors on the fringe of Celtic Gaul, have to be mentioned. The first was Armorica (the region situated to the north of the Loire and the west of the Seine) which was dominated by the Veneti. The tribes in this coastal region were traditionally sea-going and did a certain amount of trade with the Island of Britain. The Viducassi, refugees from Belgium, occupied the most eastern part of Armorica. To the south of the Loire, on the Atlantic coast, the Andecaves, Turones, Pictones, Santones, Lemovices and Petrocorii made up the last sector which was as big as it was sparsely populated.

Finally in south-west Gaul, Aquitania formed a separate area where, like the neighbouring Roman province, Celts and Ligures mingled more or less evenly. This region had remained aloof from the Arverni's and the Bituriges' attempts at domination during the preceding centuries, whilst being very much influenced by the Celtiberi, settled on the other side of the Pyrenees.

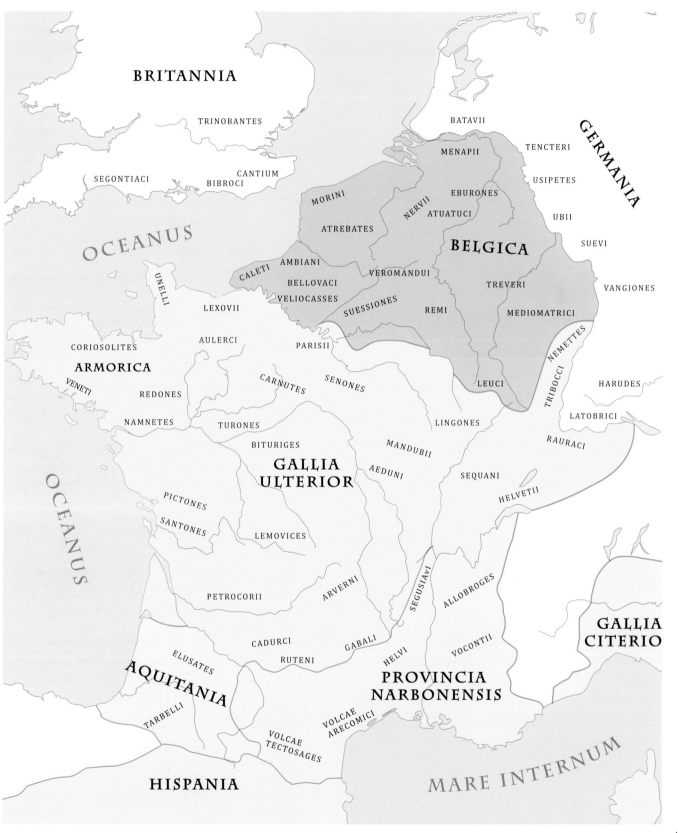

BRITANNIA

TRINOBANTES

SEGONTIACI

CANTIUM
BIBROCI

OCEANUS

BATAVII

MENAPII

GERMANIA

TENCTERI

USIPETES

MORINI

EBURONES

UBII

ATREBATES

NERVII

ATUATUCI

SUEVI

BELGICA

VANGIONES

UNELLI

CALETI

AMBIANI

BELLOVACI

VELIOCASSES

VEROMANDUI

TREVERI

LEXOVII

SUESSIONES

REMI

MEDIOMATRICI

CORIOSOLITES

AULERCI

PARISII

NEMETTES

HARUDES

ARMORICA

SENONES

LEUCI

TRIBOCCI

VENETI

CARNUTES

LATOBRICI

REDONES

LINGONES

RAURACI

NAMNETES

TURONES

MANDUBII

OCEANUS

BITURIGES

GALLIA
ULTERIOR

AEDUNI

SEQUANI

HELVETII

PICTONES

SANTONES

LEMOVICES

ARVERNI

SEGUSIAVI

ALLOBROGES

GALLIA
CITERIO

PETROCORII

CADURCI

GABALI

HELVI

VOCONTII

ELUSATES

RUTENI

AQUITANIA

PROVINCIA
NARBONENSIS

TARBELLI

VOLCAE
ARECOMICI

VOLCAE
TECTOSAGES

HISPANIA

MARE INTERNUM

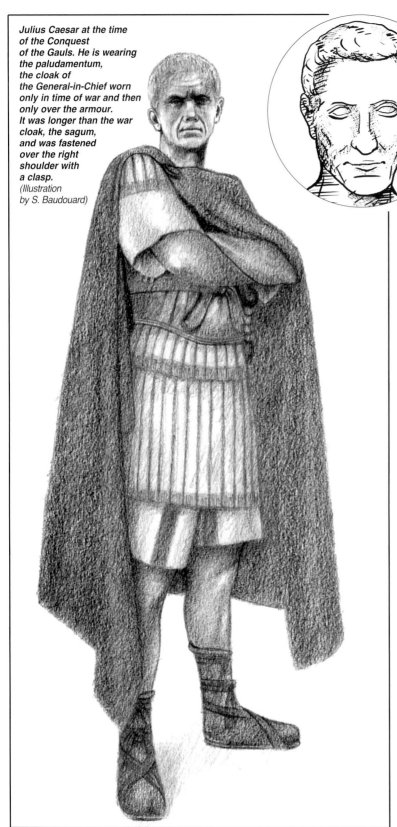

Julius Caesar at the time of the Conquest of the Gauls. He is wearing the paludamentum, the cloak of the General-in-Chief worn only in time of war and then only over the armour. It was longer than the war cloak, the sagum, and was fastened over the right shoulder with a clasp.
(Illustration by S. Baudouard)

Detail from a bronze statue of Julius Caesar. Renderings of the Roman general are rare at the time and the statues showing him, or rather glorifying him, are from after the conquest of Gaul. (RR)

Aquilifer (eagle bearer) from the Xth Legion at the time Caesar's army landed in Brittany. The standard bearer was chosen for his courage and loyalty to his unit. His shield was smaller than the legionaries' because it was easier to handle. He is carrying the eagle, the legion's insignia. The aquilifer is wearing the traditional bear - leopard - or wolf-skin, as here.
(Illustration by Mark Churms)

THE AEDUI AT THE CENTRE OF THE GAULS' POLITICAL EQUILIBRIUM

In 60 BC, the Aedui, encouraged by their alliance with Rome seemed to dominate independent Gaul. The Arverni had renounced their claim to a dominant position for the time being. Only the Sequani, a tribe settled between the Saône and the Jura seemed to question the status quo of the time.

Be that as it may, Gaul's political structures were more or less in full decline. Each tribe, jealous of its independence, was controlled by an oligarchy made up of nobles. The latter - landowners and military chiefs -reinforced their position by using the services of a clientele in which the *"ambactes"*- vassals - were a separate category.

These were soldiers of servile rank and were like a caste whose calling was purely military. The people themselves, be they *non-noble* Gauls or assimilated pre-Celtic populations, were in a most precarious situation. In the years preceding the Gallic Wars they had become very much impoverished.

Moreover, at the time there was no permanent Gallic army nor for that matter was it in any way unified. In the event of a conflict, each tribe assembled its contingents which fought autonomously, in ranks behind their chieftains. For the Gallic troops, the strike force was based on its cavalry which was made up of nobles, their direct clients and their vassals. This cavalry wore a coat of mail or leather armour and a metal helmet. They fought with lances or swords and outclassed their Roman counterparts as usual. The infantry made up the bulk of the warriors and assembled levies of non-professional warriors conscripted for the duration of a campaign. These soldiers were fitted out with a shield, a sword and a pike. Like all Gauls, these infantrymen were brave and fierce fighters, but they were not at all organised tactically, nothing like the Roman cohorts. The Belgian tribes were an exception to this overall state of affairs. With them the cavalry did not play such an important role. On the other hand their infantry still possessed the

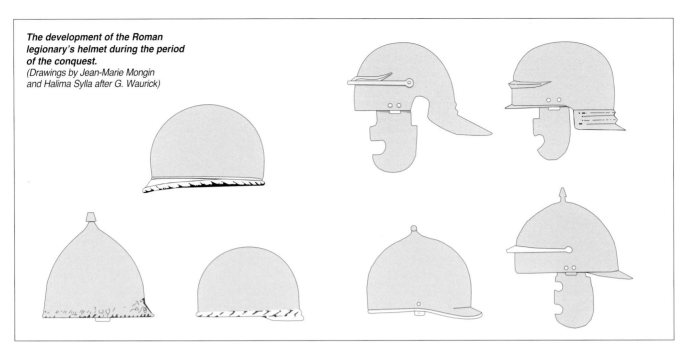

The development of the Roman legionary's helmet during the period of the conquest.
(Drawings by Jean-Marie Mongin and Halima Sylla after G. Waurick)

Following page, right.
Obverse and reverse sides of a Roman sesterce.
(Reconstitution, Private Collection, RR)

Below.
The liberality of Luernos, a Gallic chieftain largely "subsidised" by the Romans. War was not the only way to conquer peoples' souls or to obtain their good favours.
(Illustration by H de Nolhac, Private Collection)

Gauls' age-old courage from the days when they made Rome tremble. Finally, although the quality of the Gauls' weapons was generally very good, army logistics and supplies were left up to each individual warrior.

THE ROMAN REPUBLIC IS RENT APART

The first part of the 1st century AD is one of the most agitated periods in the history of the Roman Republic. Rome's good fortune can only astonish: *"Torn apart by social conflicts of unbelievable fierceness, threatened by powerful enemies and engaged in dangerous expansionist wars, how had this little town of shepherds, exiles and adventurers become the metropolis whose control over the known world was to last more than a thousand years?"* What is more, the four decades between 100 and 60 BC seemed

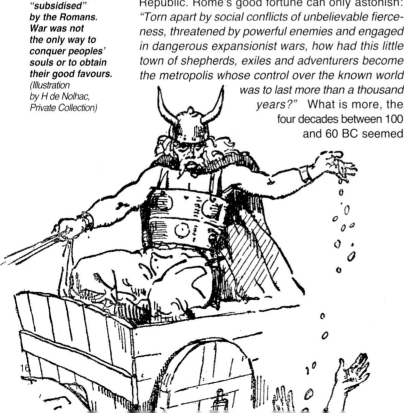

to concentrate all the ills imaginable which could have overcome the city's fortunes. After 102 BC and his great victory over the Cimbri and the Teutones, Caius Marius, the figurehead of the Populares ("people's party"), imposed his authority on the Roman government. During the following years however his rivalry with the leader of the Optimates (the "aristocratic party") Lucius Cornelius Sulla degenerated into out-and-out civil war. Marius was a consul for a total of seven times, being sometimes chased out of Rome by Sulla's partisans sometimes summoned back to the town, until he died in 86 BC. Sulla who overcame the late Marius' supporters in 82 BC, imposed a three-year dictatorship. He carried out bloody purges, putting 90 senators and 2600 knights to death. At the same time between 91 and 89 BC, the Republic had to deal with a revolt started by its Italian allies during the terrible "Social War" (from socii, allies). It ended with Rome making concessions including granting citizenship to its Italian allies. In 88 BC after the *"Ephesian Vespers"* in which 80 000 Roman citizens in Asia Minor were murdered, the Republic had to commit itself and both fight Mithridates, the King of Pontus, and at the same time deal with this civil war that was wreaking havoc.

After Sulla's self-imposed abdication in 79 BC, many different leaders emerged. Pompey for the Optimates got rid of the last of Marius' followers, assembled under Sertorius' command in Spain. Then there was the great slaves' rebellion led by Spartacus which put Italy to fire and the sword between 73 and 71 BC. Marcus Licinius Crassus finally crushed Spartacus' army and colluded with Pompey to take up the posi-

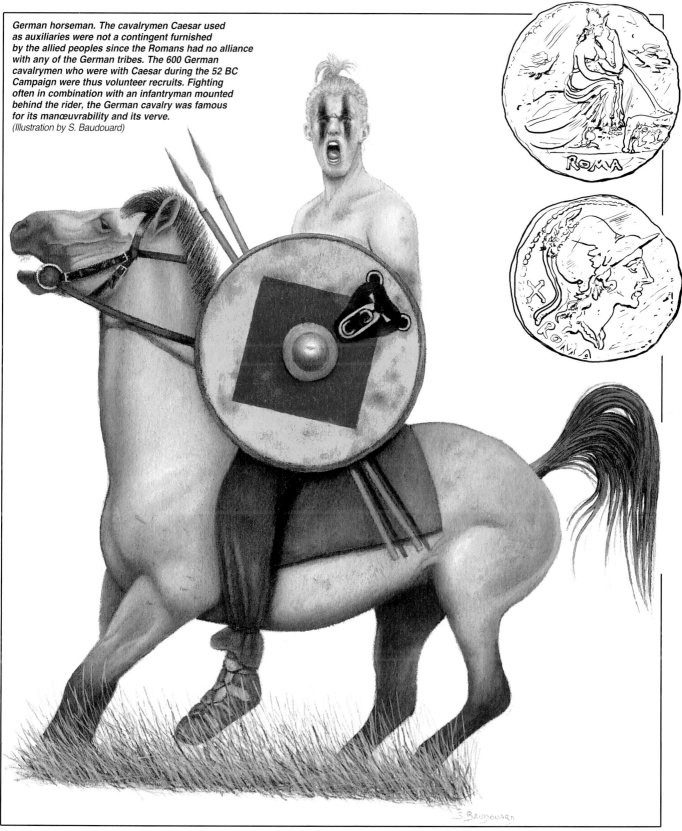

German horseman. The cavalrymen Caesar used as auxiliaries were not a contingent furnished by the allied peoples since the Romans had no alliance with any of the German tribes. The 600 German cavalrymen who were with Caesar during the 52 BC Campaign were thus volunteer recruits. Fighting often in combination with an infantryman mounted behind the rider, the German cavalry was famous for its manœuvrability and its verve.
(Illustration by S. Baudouard)

17

Vue du Puy d'Issolu prise du côté du midi

tion of consul in 70 BC. The two men then dominated public life. In 63 BC a new conjuration, Catilina's, shook the Republic but this was put down notably thanks to Cicero who was then consul and who reacted vigorously.

Meanwhile, Pompey had established his reputation as one of the great generals by subjugating the East and bringing it under Rome's law. It was also at about this time that Julius Caesar entered Rome's political arena, taking up the torch of the People's Party, since he was related to Marius' family. In 60 BC Pompey, Caesar and Crassus put together a mutual support agreement which was soon known as the First Triumvirate. This partnership led to Caesar's first consulate in 59 BC.

THE RISE OF CAESAR

Caius Julius Caesar came from the prestigious family of the Julii. This made him theoretically a descendant of Iule, the son of Aeneas of Troy, himself the son of Anchises and the goddess Venus. Caesar often referred to this divine origin: *"My Aunt Julia came down from kings through the family of her mother and is related to the immortal gods by that of her father."* [4] Rather more down to earth, his family tree as it is known to us only goes back two or three centuries.

Julius Caesar was born on 13 July, either in 101 BC or in 100 BC; he was a nephew of Marius which was very important in the political context of the time. Caesar's career was dazzling. *"Caesar was a brilliant young aristocrat, who had dared to marry the daughter of Cin-*

na the democrat, who then refused to obey Sulla who called upon him to repudiate her. On this occasion, although reluctantly bowing down to the Vestals' intercessions in favour of this stubborn offspring of the gens Julia, he had said:* "Even though I sense that he is quickened by a multitude of Mariuses, you may do what you wish with him".* At the death of Sulla, the rising star called Caesar began cutting corners in the cursus honorum - quaestor, aedile, praetor, consul – and very quickly imposed his personality on the highest levels of Roman political life until he became, he a noble, the chief of the Populares."* [5] One of the most striking events of his young career was the lavish series of games he organised to honour his father who disappeared in Rome in 65 BC whilst he was curule aedile. He clearly made himself very popular with the plebs, but also ran up just as astonishing debts. Caesar also got good experience when he served as quaestor (in 69 BC), then as praetor (61 BC) in the province of Hispania. It was however when he became Pontifex Maximus in 62 BC that Caesar was given the biggest responsibility which was to be had. Caesar's consulate from 59 BC onwards, the fruit of a political agreement with Pompey and Crassus, showed how generally effective the triumvirate could be ruling the Republic. Thanks to support from his allies, Caesar could show how active he could be: the agrarian laws, a treaty with Ptolemy III's Egypt, for instance.

Caesar's inexorable rise continued. Braving the Senate's caginess when the time came to vote on who was to be allotted which province, *"the triumviral machine calmly got under way. The tribune Valentinius had a plebiscite passed before the people entrusting Caesar with Cisalpine Gaul (Northern Italy) and Illyricum for five years. He would have three legions at his disposition, would choose his legates himself and could establish colonies. Meanwhile, the former consul, Quintus Metellus Celer, who had been sent to Transalpine Gaul (Southern Gaul), died. (...) The Senate, no doubt wishing to blow with the prevailing wind, added the governorship of Transalpine Gaul and a fourth legion to Caesar's 'package'"*. [6] Being

Above, from left to right.
The Puy d'Issolu, the probable site of the battle of Uxellodunum during the expedition against Drappes and Lucterios in 51 BC.
(Atlas belonging to Napoleon III, Private Collection)

Below.
Gallic horseman.
(Private Collection, RR)

Opposite.
A fight during one of the many sieges which the Romans set up during the War against the Gauls.
(Lithography by Joliet for one of the editions of the "Gallic Wars" by Julius Caesar. RR. Private Collection)

Far right.
Gallic Chieftain.
(Private Collection, RR)

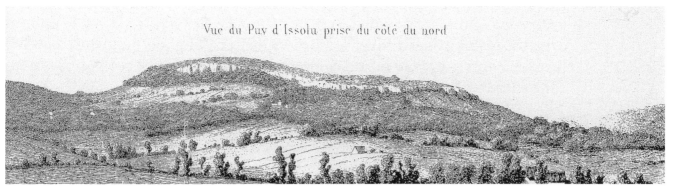

Vue du Puy d'Issolu prise du côté du nord

given a province just after obtaining a consulate allowed Caesar to benefit from the immunity which went with the job and he thereby escaped the accusations and lawsuits which his political enemies in the aristocracy were preparing to throw at him. The same year, so as to reinforce the already solid links between the two men, Pompey married Julia, Caesar's daughter and Caesar himself remarried, this time Calpurnia, the daughter of Lucius Calpurnius Pison, an influential member of the Nobilitas, elected consul for the following year. While Caesar was getting ready to leave for his province, with the legal proviso that he could not return to Rome before the end of his five-year term, Pompey looked after his veterans and Crassus, the banker for the triumvirate, reorganised his affairs. In Rome Clodius, who had become the tribune for the Plebs, managed to get the triumvirate's most prominent adversaries out of Rome: at first Cato, then later Cicero. After setting up his *"intelligence networks"* in the town, Caesar set off for Cisalpine Gaul quite determined to enhance his reputation and power by using the circumstances, whatever they might be. On the brink financially, he was also counting on reimbursing his enormous debts, *"for Caesar, war was a sort of relentless flight to escape from the courts and his creditors, and protect himself from his ruthless opponents."* [7]

GAUL'S INEVITABLE SUBJUGATION

Was Caesar actually thinking of conquering Gaul while it was still independent?
His immediate objective was no doubt to become as eminent as Pompey.
Despite his rapid political rise to power, the new proconsul
of Cisalpine Gaul, Transalpine Gaul and Illyricum was less prominent
than his two partners in the first triumvirate.
Crassus had defeated Spartacus and Pompey had put down
the Orient and Spain. Caesar was still nothing where military glory was concerned.
To improve his popularity, nothing would be more effective than
to get hold of loot and slaves during a war of conquest.

Below.
Julius Caesar at the head of his legions during the 52 BC campaign.
(Illustration by H de Nolhac, Private Collection)

CÆSAR

WITH THIS IN MIND, THE PROCONSUL had two options open to him: an expedition towards the Danube, against the Rhetii, the Taurici or the Scordiscii who occupied the land between Caesar's provinces and that great river; or an advance through Gaul up to the Rhine.

But in order push the frontiers of the Roman Republic back even further, there had to be a good excuse, an opportunity he could exploit so that he didn't waste time conjecturing.

THE GERMAN "THREAT", ARIOVISTUS AND THE HELVETII

In Book I of his *Bellum Gallicum*, Caesar *a posteriori* justified the need for his meddling in Gaul's affairs by repeating a speech made by an Aedui druid, sent as an ambassador to Rome, probably in 61 BC to plead his tribe's cause. The man, Diviciac, developed the following argument: the Aedui had been Rome's allies for a long time; the Arverni, already beaten by the legions in 125-120 BC were no longer a menace; on the other hand the Sequani, also friends of the Republic since Marius' period, were now the Aedui's open rivals; finally the Sequani apparently had appealed to trans-Rhine Germans for help in dominating Gaul.

The most important point in all this was the reference to Ariovistus, the German chieftain with a strangely Gallic-sounding name who now set himself up as arbiter between the most powerful Gallic tribes. Now it just so happened that Caesar had honoured this same Ariovistus with the title of "King and Friend of the Romans" justified no doubt by his desire to win over some allies along the Rhine in case he had to make an expedition on the Danube.

However that may be, Divciac's speech, reported and therefore not a little "arranged", indicated one

BY ROME'S LEGIONS

thing at least: that Gallic living space was under a certain pressure from the Germans. The fact that Ariovistus had been invited by the Sequani or come to Gaul on his own initiative does seem to have worried the Celts, who had less and less faith in their own military muscle. Besides, where the mention of Diviciac's deputation would appear to be the most calculating concerns the actual event which drove Caesar to penetrate Gaul with his legions, since in 58 BC it was no longer the future of the Aedui that preoccupied the governor of Transalpine Gaul, but the Helvetii's massive migration along its border, of which he had just been notified. The Helvetii were a powerful tribe living in present-day Switzerland but they had just decided to move with wives, children and baggage to the Atlantic coast, into Santones territory where there didn't seem to be many men. Why such an expedition? Once again the pressure of the Germans could be felt behind this move. Was it because the proximity of the Germans was becoming more and more of a burden on the Helvetii's security and prosperity that they started looking for clearer horizons elsewhere? The only problem for the poor Helvetii was that their undertaking could not go unnoticed (there were about 300 000 of them in all), neither could it fail to remind the Romans of that bad period when the Cimbri and the Teutones also migrated. In Rome's subconscious, the Helvetii moving around could only be a bad thing and it had to be prevented.

More prosaically in Caesar's mind, it was a golden opportunity to take a major part in independent Gaul's affairs. Even though Caesar later unsuccessfully claimed that this migration had been planned several years earlier by Orgetorix, the chief of the Helvetii, in a sort of plot aimed at ruining the Allobroges' lands (part of the Transalpine Gaul province) and taking

over inner Gaul, it is rather difficult to imagine that his reaction was not dictated by the emergency of this *a contrario* unforeseen situation. To sum up: Caesar was waiting. He was hesitating between seeing to the Danube region or dealing with Gaul, in order to coax the fortunes of war.

He readied his allies far and wide, played on all the fronts - political, diplomatic and military - while waiting for the right opportunity. The Helvetii's migration upset his most elabo-

Opposite, left.
The German chieftain Arriovistus.
(Illustration by H de Nolhac, Private Collection)

Roman legionary and Gallic warrior locked in single combat.
(Illustration by G. Rava, © Vae Victis 2006)

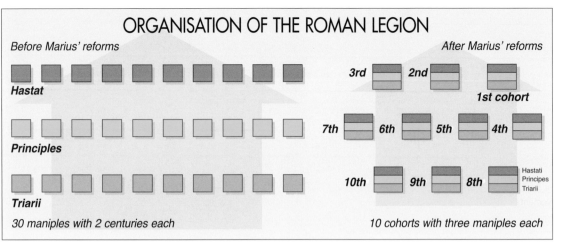

ORGANISATION OF THE ROMAN LEGION

Before Marius' reforms

Hastat

Principles

Triarii

30 maniples with 2 centuries each

After Marius' reforms

3rd 2nd

1st cohort

7th 6th 5th 4th

10th 9th 8th Hastati / Principes / Triarii

10 cohorts with three maniples each

Opposite.
The disposition of the Roman legion in combat before and after Marius' reforms in the 1st century BC.
(Sketch by Halima Sylla and Jean-Marie Mongin)

Opposite.
Julius Caesar's campaigns during the Gallic Wars.
(Map by Antoine Poggioli and Jean-Marie Mongin)

rate plans but it worried Rome so much more that it was only natural for him to react. It was only after the war that Caesar tried to give a plausible explanation for the course of events which did more justice to his political genius.

For the time being, there was one thing preoccupying him: how do you stop a whole nation from moving when it has burnt its villages to persuade itself never to return, with only four legions?

CAESAR'S ARMY

Julius Caesar inherited an army which had been through a decisive change fifty years earlier. Traditionally Rome had always relied for its defence on a citizens' army, coming from the propertied classes, recruited for a single war or campaign. Originally the legionaries had to pay for their equipment themselves and only earned a pittance.

Over the centuries with wars separating Roman soldiers from their homes and for longer periods, recruitment became more and more difficult.

All the conscripts thought about was getting back to their farms and their families. A thorough reform of the military system soon became necessary. Indeed, at the end of the 2nd century BC, as the war against

Jugurtha in Africa dragged on and became unpopular, it became almost impossible to recruit anybody. Marius who at the time was in charge of things, completely revolutionised the Roman army.

Marius' reforms first concerned where the recruits came from. He got rid of any notions of wealth and enrolled all the poor volunteers who turned up. It was only the pay that interested them and long service did not bother them. Service also enabled them to save money which could open up another life for them once they were freed.

Marius had put together a truly permanent army made up of professionals. Pay was increased; the offensive and defensive weapons were mass produced thereby costing less so that every soldier was equipped like only the Triarii (a veterans' unit kept in reserve) were at the time of the Republic. The Velites, light troops who operated in front of the army at this moment in history, now disappeared.

The new legions were now organised in cohorts made up of legionaries all armed in the same way with a long sword (70-75 cm) and a pilum (javelin). The pilum, which was the Romans' favourite throwing weapon, was about two metres long.

The long iron consisted of a thin shaft ending with a pyramidal point which was particularly sharp. The thinness of the iron, combined with the wooden shaft, made it bend under the impact, preventing the enemy from reusing it.

Each legion now comprised ten cohorts each bringing together three former manipules (companies): one of hastate (pike-men), one of principes and one of triarii - soldiers from the three classes of fighters used earlier but now abolished. These cohorts were usually deployed as on a checker-board, in three echelons.

Below.
Gallic runners galloping to break through the Roman lines in order to get their messages to the besieged troops.
(Illustration by H. de Nolhac, Private Collection)

BRITANNIA

OCEANUS

ARMORICA

VENÈTES

GALLIA
ULTERIOR

OCEANUS

AQUITANIA

HISPANIA

German attacks
Roman movements
Battles

54 BC

Portius Itius
(Boulogne)
55 BC.

Samarobriva
(Amiens)

57 BC

Noviodunum
(Soissons)

Genabum
(Orléans)

56 BC

P. Crassus
58 BC

Défaite de Usipètes
et Tenctères
55 BC

Aduatuca
(Tongres)

GERMANIA

55 BC

BELGICA

57 av. J.-C.

ARIOVISTE

58 BC

HELVÈTES

Bibracte
(Mt Beuvray)

Vesontio
(Besançon

Défaite
Helvète
58 BC.

GALLIA
CITERIOR

PROVINCIA
NARBONENSIS

Narbo Martius
(Narbonne)

Massalia
(Marseille)

MARE INTERNUM

23

Above.
The representatives of the Rhemi arriving among their allies.
(Illustration by H. de Nolhac, Private Collection)

Below.
Roman legionary.
(Illustration by G. Rava, © Vae Victis 2006)

With citizenship extended after the Social War to all those Italians living south of the River Pô, there were no longer any "allied" legions or "citizens' legions but simply "Roman" legions. Finally, to complete his reforms Marius made the army more mobile by getting rid of the heavy baggage trains which inevitably slowed it down. He decided that each legionary would carry his own belongings and a few days' rations on his back. The Roman soldiers very quickly earned the nickname of "Marius' mules" as their fate as beasts of burdens did seem so unenviable. The changes were less obvious in the officer corps. In Caesar's time, each legion was commanded by six tribunes, from the nobility. The rank of legate, the real general commanding the legion was nevertheless created once again to make the army's organisation more professional.

THE HELVETII ARE CRUSHED AND THE ELIMINATION OF ARIOVISTUS

In 59 BC, Julius Caesar had only the four legions assigned to his pro-consular province: the VIIth, VIIIth, IXth and Xth. Three of these legions were billeted at Aquileia and the fourth was probably stationed in Roman Gaul, near Narbo. The Xth was made up of the most war-hardened veterans and was considered as the elite unit in this army; Caesar had absolute faith in it right from the outset of the campaign. In 58 BC, at his own expense the proconsul recruited two new units in Cisalpine Gaul, the XIth and XIIth legions.

With about 5 000 men per legion, at the start his army numbered some 30 000 men to which have to be added several auxiliary units: Cretan archers, Balearic slingers, Numidian light infantry and Roman or Gallic (from the allied tribes) cavalry. The number of servants and slaves following in the army's wake was almost as high as the number of soldiers themselves.

It was in March 58 BC that a long column of 300 000 people, mainly Helvetii, accompanied by Boii, Raurarci from Tulingii and Latovicii set off in a westerly direction. It assembled near Geneva, an Allobroge city and part of the Roman province. Caesar hurried to Geneva by forced march and ordered the single legion on the spot to cut the bridge over the Rhone. Unable to cross the river, the Helvetii persuaded the Aedui chief, Dumnorix, to allow them to cross Aedui and Sequani territory to reach Western Gaul.

On his return to Cisalpine Gaul, Caesar levied the two legions already mentioned and marched in pursuit of the Helvetii who entered Celtic Gaul through Ambibarii territory. Caesar moved up along the left bank of the Saône and crushed the Helvetii's rearguard which had not yet crossed the river. He had the legionaries make a bridge and crossed the river, catching up with the enemy column near Bibracte, in Aedui territory, at the beginning of June. To oppose his 40 000 men, the Helvetii could only field a smaller force, some 20 to 30 000 men according Hans Delbrück). Caesar had his four legions in the front line and kept the two freshly-recruited legions in reserve guarding the camp. With them he left the Aedui auxiliaries who had just joined him and whom he did not really trust.

The Helvetii attacked but the legions whose tactical discipline worked marvellously easily drove them off then launched a terrible counter-attack. The carnage which followed reached the carts carrying the women and children of the migrating tribes and was horrible. After disarming the survivors and demanding hostages, Caesar sent the Helvetii and their allies back towards the villages which they had burnt down just before they left!

The Helvetii were not the only ones to threaten Gaul's stability. Some Germans had crossed the Rhine with their chief Ariovistus to settle definitively on the left bank. The Sequani who had initially counted on using the Germans as a foundation for their hegemony were on the defensive from now on. Impressed by Caesar's victory near Bibracte, they appealed to the Roman Proconsul to get rid of Ariovistus for them. He needed no prompting: with his army he marched against Vesontio (Besançon), the capital of the Sequani. He sojourned there for several days to re-supply. These few days of inactivity provoked a certain amount of fear and panic among the legions at the idea not only of fighting the Germans who were said to be invincible, but also of penetrating so far north into lands where no legionaries had ever set foot. Caesar was not one to let himself be impressed. He told his legionaries that he was going to fight the Germans, with or without them, taking with him the most valiant cohorts who wanted to follow him: *"If now nobody followed him, he'd march on regardless, followed by the Xth of whom he was sure and*

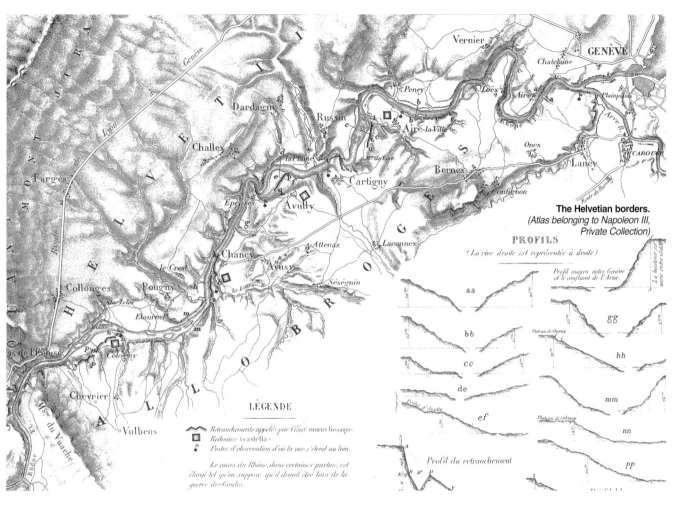

The Helvetian borders.
(Atlas belonging to Napoleon III, Private Collection)

LÉGENDE

Retranchements appelés par César murus fossaque.
Redoutes (castella)
Postes d'observation d'où la vue s'étend au loin.

Le cours du Rhône, dans certaines parties, est élargi tel qu'on suppose qu'il devait être lors de la guerre des Gaules.

PROFILS
(La rive droite est représentée à droite)

whom he would use as his Praetorian cohort."[8] Fear changed to enthusiasm in the presence of such a leader and the entire army took up the march northwards. The encounter with Ariovistus took place to the south of the Alsatian plain. The Germans at first had the advantage of mobility: their cavalry, who carried lightly armed infantrymen mounted behind the rider, managed to threaten the Roman supply lines for a moment. But the battle had to be joined and be done with. When Ariovistus was finally forced to stand and fight, he forewent the mobility of his troops and filled out his ranks with his light troops to hide the fact that he was out-numbered.

The Germans nonetheless went over to the attack and Caesar's left wing almost yielded. The proconsul had to engage his third echelon to meet the emergency and drive back the enemy attack. In the end the legions' steadfastness got the better of German furia and Ariovistus' front line finished by yielding, the Romans pushed home their advantage and attacked the Germans' camp where the carts were used as barricades. Caesar's victory was total. Ariovistus fled back over the Rhine and was never heard of again.

When setting himself up as the "liberator of Gaul" against the *"invading Germans",*

Below
The Carnute chieftains lead their troops into battle.
(Illustration by H. de Nolhac, Private Collection)

25

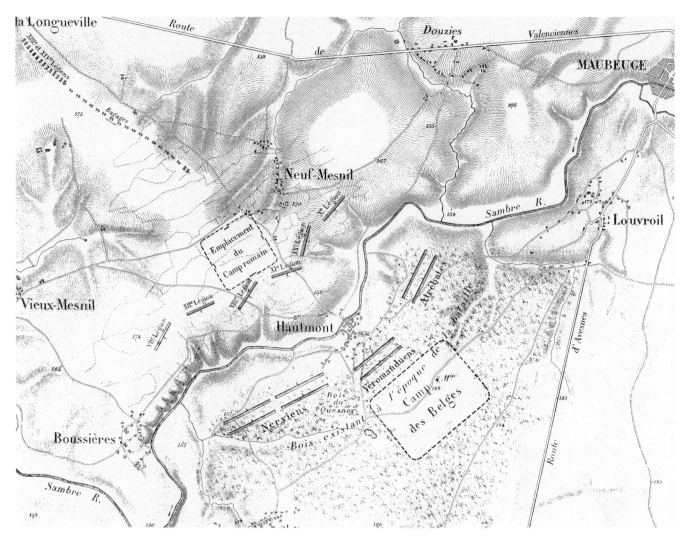

Caesar had gambled heavily but won. He could legitimately settle in Celtic Gaul. The legions indeed set up their winter quarters between Vesontio and the Rhine. In Caesar's mind, it was clear on his return to Cisalpine Gaul that only permanent occupation of Gaul by the Romans would secure a lasting peace and also, indirectly, guarantee lasting security for Transalpine Gaul and Cisalpine Gaul.

VICTORY OVER THE BELGIANS

The fact that Caesar's legions wintered in Gaul very soon started to worry the neighbouring tribes in Belgian Gaul who during the winter of 58-57 BC began preparing for war. Caesar also brought in reinforcements: he levied another two legions in Cisalpine Gaul, once again at his expense.

These were the XIIIth and XIVth legions who brought legionary strength up to 40 000 men. Playing as was his wont on the divisions between the Gallic tribes, the proconsul tried hard to stir up rivalries by winning over the Rhemi who would thenceforth be his most faithful allies.

He then sent his Aedui contingents to the limits of Belgian Gaul as a diversion.

Above:
The Battle of the Sambre between the Belgians and the Romans.
(Atlas belonging to Napoleon III, Private Collection)

The warring Gauls did not hesitate to carry out a scorched earth policy to delay the advance of Caesar's legions.
(Illustration by H. de Nolhac, Private Collection)

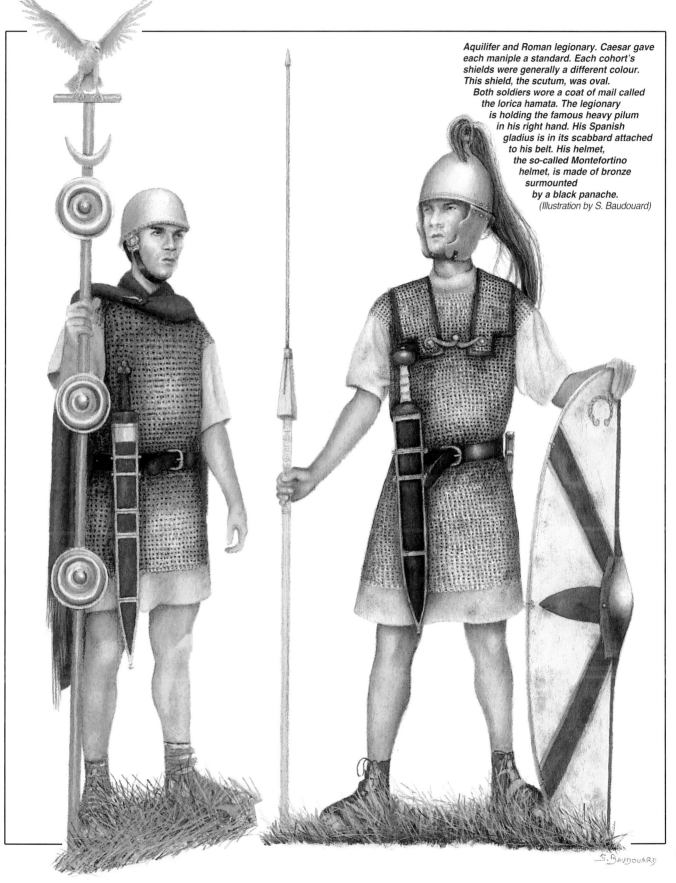

Aquilifer and Roman legionary. Caesar gave each maniple a standard. Each cohort's shields were generally a different colour. This shield, the scutum, was oval.
Both soldiers wore a coat of mail called the lorica hamata. The legionary is holding the famous heavy pilum in his right hand. His Spanish gladius is in its scabbard attached to his belt. His helmet, the so-called Montefortino helmet, is made of bronze surmounted by a black panache.
(Illustration by S. Baudouard)

When Caesar, at the head of his army all gathered in one column, broke deeply into Belgian territory, he found facing him only a coalition of three tribes: Nervii, Viromanuenes and Atrebates. The decisive battle took place on the Sambre, and although Caesar speaks of a Belgian army of 300 000 men in the Bellum Gallicum, Hans Delbrück thinks that the army led by the Nervii was no doubt no bigger than the Roman army. Whatever, the fight was terrible since the *"bravest of these three peoples (Aquitanii, Gauls and Belgians) were the Belgians, because they were the furthest from the Roman* province *and the least influenced by its civilisation (...) and finally because they were nearest to the Germans who lived on the other side of the Rhine and with whom they were continually fighting. It was for the same reason that the Helvetii also outdid the other Gauls in valour."* [9] The great battle took place near the Sambre. Caesar lined up eight legions (40 000 men) this time. Things almost turned out badly because the Gauls attacked the Roman vanguard while the soldiers were still busy building their camp.

The Romans had not had the time to take up their usual formidable combat deployment and two legions were indeed still marching up, quite some way from the battlefield. Cool-headedly Caesar managed to check the furious Belgian attack on the camp and gradually re-establish the situation. Once again the iron discipline which prevailed in his army enabled him to re-form a solid battle line. The Nervii contingent and its chief Buduognatos managed to take the Roman camp, routing the auxiliaries and seriously threatening the VIIth and XIIth Legions on Caesar's right wing. Once again the Xth Legion played a determining role by being at the most exposed sectors of the front. Finally the late arrival of the XIIIth and XIVth Legions, whose first campaign it was, finally tipped the scales in Caesar's favour. Caesar sent his legate Labenius to command them.

The Roman counter-offensive was terrible; the Belgians, attacked from the rear, were slaughtered. Of the 60 000 combatants lined up, Caesar states that only 500 were able to escape safe and sound. This total victory opened the gates to the rest of Belgian Gaul for Caesar. The Suessiones and the Bellovaci had already agreed to submit to the Romans before the battle; they now moved into the territories of the three tribes vanquished at the

Battle of the Sambre and got hold of their oppida. The Romans took the fighting to the fierce Eburones and Atuatuci who, in spite of their initial resolution to fight to the death, also ended up by submitting to Caesar's law.

A PACIFICATION STRATEGY

In two campaigns and three set battles against peoples supposed to be the most valiant in Gaul, Caesar had done away with his most dangerous adversaries. His move along the eastern borders of the country (Jura, Rhine and Belgium) hemmed in the heart of Celtic Gaul, stunning the Gauls with the extent of his successes.

The victory on the Sambre thus marked the end of the period of the great set-piece battles. From now on the war against the Gauls took on a new aspect, that of pacification. Caesar's new strategy was founded on several principles: having the legions winter in the centre of Gaul, actively orchestrating the Gauls' political divisions, conducting siege operations, using certain forms of "counter-guerrilla" operations to fight against the "little war" which the isolated Gallic tribes, incapable of confronting the legions in open country were trying to impose and finally on the borders, intimidating the Gauls' potential allies.

On the other hand the political situation in Rome was getting rather complicated for Caesar. Cicero was back in the capital during the winter of 57-56 BC, after three years governing the province of Africa. Caesar had agreed to this return though this did not prevent Cicero from attacking the proconsul in the Senate in the spring. The triumvirs, Crassus, Pompey and Caesar met at Lucques to coordinate their response. They decided that the first two would be candidates for the consulate in 55 BC and then back a prolongation of Caesar's mandate in Gaul. Pompey was given the task of calming Cicero's zeal petitioning against Caesar. Strengthened by these new assurances Caesar left Cisalpine Gaul and returned to internal Gaul.

Between 56 and 53 BC the pacification policy envisaged by Caesar was pursued without any great hitches. 56 BC was spent in the west of Gaul. Caesar, with the majority of his forces, invaded Armorica. He captured the oppida of the tribes who resisted him one by one. He then divided his army. Three legions were sent to present-day Normandy to the Unelli, Curiosolites and Lexovii. Caesar hurried with the other legions to the territory of the region's most powerful tribe, the Venetii, who relied on a long sea-going tradition to defy the Romans on the seas.

Caesar did not allow himself to be intimidated. In a matter of weeks he had his soldiers build a fleet entirely on the Loire and put Decimus Brutus in command of it. Even though they had been built accor-

ding to designs for ships sailing calm seas like the Mediterranean, he put his galleys to sea to defy the Venetii on their own ground, or rather sea. With the good fortune of the daring, Caesar succeeded in beating the Gauls' fleet of high-sided sailing vessels by using a moment of windless sea which halted his opponents. The resourcefulness of his engineers did the rest: scythes attached to long poles cut the Venetii's rigging, paralysing them once and for all. The legionaries then only had to storm the ships.

Meanwhile the legate Publius Crassus, the triumvir's son, put down Aquitania with a single legion for the cost of a few clashes which all turned out in his favour.

THE ROMAN ARMY CONSOLIDATED

Over the following three years (55-53 BC) the general trend was stepped up. Caesar no longer had to carry out any large-scale operations and took no further risks. He sent his cavalry and legionaries to plunder the farms and ravage the lands of the tribes who refused to submit. In rather a surprising way, it was now the Roman army which carried out guerrilla operations on a large scale to overrun

Below.
These Gauls are straight from German popular imagination. On this side of the Rhine, they could be taken for Germans if it were not for the "Celtic" motif printed on the woman's dress.
(Private Collection, RR)

Gaul. The Gauls who tried to resist were quickly forced to seek refuge in their strongholds and the Romans always managed to get them to surrender. Thanks to the quality of their engineers and the professionalism of their technique and siege machines (assault ramps, siege towers, battering rams, gallery mining, etc.) Caesar's troops got the better of a hundred or so oppida all during the war. During these same years, the proconsul took advantage of the relative calm which reigned in Gaul to cross over to Britannia (present-day England) twice and to cross the Rhine twice. These operations were limited in time and in scope, but they gave Caesar certain advantages. From a political point of view, in Rome they increased the prestige of a general who overcame natural obstacles which no Roman before him had ever dared to do. From a military standpoint, these expeditions cut Gaul off a bit more from its outside surroundings and further reinforced the lasting nature of the Roman occupation. The Gauls themselves were disconcerted: by crossing the Channel or by building a bridge over the Rhine, Caesar let it be understood that his hands weren't tied, that the Gauls' capacity to challenge his authority was negligible and that he had already set about pre-emptively defending the borders of his new conquests.

The Romans now had a firm hold over Gaul. All the more so since Caesar continually reinforced his eight legion-strong army with a number of allied contingents. From 57 BC he recruited Treviri cavalry, reputed for being the best in all

Gaul. The proconsul could also count on the Rhemi and the Aedui, his most faithful allies to back him both for supplies and information. Back-up troops from Transalpine Gaul were also incorporated into his army.

After his expedition across the Rhine in 55 BC, Caesar recruited German mercenary cavalry. These soldiers, mounted on small, very robust horses turned out to be better than the Gallic auxiliaries and even the Numidian cavalry which were already serving in the proconsul's army.

SOME VERY RELATIVE FAILURES

The risk of such overwhelming domination which had resulted in all the Gallic tribes being either put down by force or recognised as Rome's allies in the autumn of 53 BC, was naturally overconfidence. On several occasions, Caesar underestimated his adversaries' capacity to react. On one occasion during the winter of 57-56 BC, a legion sent by Caesar on a special mission suffered a setback. Sent to Helvetia, Servius Sulpicius Galba, was chased by the inhabitants of Octoduros (Martigny) and the tribes of the region (Veragri and Seduni).

He had to withdraw to set up his winter quarters with the Allobroges, within the confines of the Roman province. The XIIth thereby lost control of a key mountain communication route. At the end of the same year, after his triumph over the Venetii, Caesar turned against the Menapii in northern Gaul. This time he was faced with an unexpected problem: the Gauls refused to fight and withdrew back into the forests and the marshes. The proconsul decided to cut the forest down but gave up the idea because he didn't have the time with winter setting in.

The most awkward moment for the Romans came at the end of 54 BC. After his second expedition to Britannia, Caesar placed his legions in seven winter camps, spread out over Belgian Gaul, with the intention of covering the territory and keeping a close watch over it. At the end of October most likely, the Eburones started a rebellion. They marched against the remotest Roman camp located on their territory. Their king, Ambiorix managed to convince the legates, Sabinius and Cotta, to abandon their camp, a fifteen-cohort garrison, promising to let them get to the nearest camps, Labenius' or Quintus Cicero's, situated further south. But this was a trap. The Eburones surrounded and attacked the legionaries once they were marching and the fifteen cohorts were all wiped out. Against the Nervii, Q. Cicero was luckier. This time the legate did not quit the camp and the attackers who had no siege materiel had to give up when they learnt of Caesar's imminent arrival with two legions as reinforcements. The following year,

BRITANNIA

GERMANIA

OCEANUS

EBURONES
✕ Aduatuca
(Tongres) 53 BC

Sicambres
53 BC

TREVERI

BELLOVAQUES

BELGICA

ARMORICA

Lutetia
(Paris)

Agedincum
(Sens) 52 BC

LINGONS

CARNUTES

Genabum
(Orléans)

Alesia
52 BC
✕

GALLIA
ULTERIOR

Avarieum
(Bourges)

ÉDUENS

Bibracte
(Mt Beuvray)

OCEANUS

Gergovie
52 BC
✕

Vienna
(Vienne)

GALLIA
CITERIOR

Uxellodunum
51 BC
✕

ARVERNI

CADURCI

AQUITANIA

PROVINCIA
NARBONENSIS

Narbo Martius
(Narbonne)

Massalia
(Marseille)

HISPANIA

MARE INTERNUM

Above.
Reconstitution of a maniple with shields,
helmet and lorica carried by the legionary in Caesar's army.
(Photograph: All Rights Reserved, Private Collection)

Opposite.
Julius Caesar at the head of his legions looking
into the future – an allegory very much in keeping
with the spirit of the 1930s.
(Illustration by H. de Nolhac, Private Collection)

after he had begun a new campaign against the Nervii and against Ambiorix, Caesar was again forced to split his army in order to close the noose around his elusive opponents. He left the baggage train at Atuatuca with a legion commanded by Q. Cicero to guard it. The brother of De Re Publica's author found himself once again under attack by hosts of Gallic and German rebels, mainly Sicambri. This time Cicero's sin was lack of caution and he only just managed to get away with it, losing 5 cohorts of recruits, 2 000 men nonetheless.

For his part, Caesar continued his work of systematic destruction according to counter-guerrilla tactics but he wasn't able to catch Ambiorix. In all Caesar lost the equivalent of two legions, always in the same circumstances: attacks on isolated camps by rebel forces that out-numbered the Romans. Each time, the Gauls had taken advantage of their mobility to outdo the proconsul. Each time the Romans returned en force to clear out the rebellious areas. To make up for his losses, Caesar was forced to recruit again in 53 BC. He used conscripts to reform the XIVth Legion, destroyed by the Eburones. Moreover, he levied *ex nihilo*, a XVth Legion and managed to get Pompey to loan him the Ist Legion which raised his total strength to ten legions.

Vercingetorix and one of his bodyguards. Unlike the traditional representations of Vercingetorix, he never wore a moustache or a horned helmet, attested by several coins bearing his effigy that have come down to us. The two men are wearing breeches, a tunic, a thick cuirass covered with a coat of mail and a surcoat with leather shoulders and a cloak fastened by clasps. The Montefortino-type helmets were made of bronze.
(Illustration by S. Baudouard)

Opposite.
**Traditional picture
— a far cry from
the reality discovered
by the latest research
— of Vercingetorix,
the young
Romanised
Gallic chieftain
in open revolt.
The hero is being
carried on a pavise
(shield), a mark
of respect reserved
for the princes
of royal blood.**
*(Illustration
by H. de Nolhac,
Private Collection)*

Opposite page.
**Vercingetorix's
childhood. The old
warriors pay homage
to the future chieftain
(top), the perfect
illustration
of the golden legend
of the young chief-
tain.** *(Illustration by
H. de Nolhac,
Private Collection)*

GENERAL REVOLT IN GAUL

Just when Gaul seemed to be completely overrun, Caesar's worries started coming from the triumvirate which had its own problems. Crassus died in 53 BC while waging war against the Parthians. What was more the death of Julia, Caesar's daughter and Pompey's wife, weakened the links between the two remaining triumvirs. Caesar proposed his ally the hand of one of his nieces and hoped thus to obtain in exchange that of Pompey's daughter (after getting the two young wives to divorce).

THIS MATRIMONIAL STRATEGY very quickly turned out to be worthless when Pompey preferred to marry Crassus' widow. Meanwhile Clodius, Caesar's man in Rome, was murdered by the partisans of another political agitator, Milo. Despite these apparently unfavourable circumstances, Pompey and Caesar made what was to be their last agreement. Pompey had Milo sentenced and obtained a dispensation for Caesar so that he could be a candidate for the consulate the following year without having to be in Rome. In exchange Caesar sent Pompey some detachments of soldiers to enable him to keep the peace in the capital. He left Ravenna with two new legions of recruits (the Vth and VIth Legions) and returned to Gaul where the latest news talked of an "insurrection".

VERCINGETORIX ARRIVES ON THE SCENE

Even after six of Julius Caesar's successive campaigns on their territory, the Gauls had not yet ruled out being free. A lot of tribal chieftains met together under the cover of the woods. Excitement mounted very quickly. Despite the defeats, they reminisced about their former military glory; vows were made to take up arms again and to fight until death or victory. There was a rather interesting strategic choice to be made. Retained in Cisalpine Gaul because of political problems in Rome, Julius Caesar had not yet returned to Celtic Gaul. The legions did not dare leave their winter quarters without their leader at

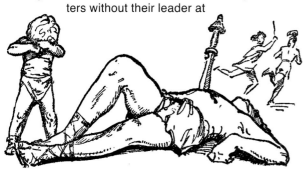

their head. The Gauls therefore hoped that a general insurrection might cut off the Roman legions from their general. The Carnutes were the most virulent. They swore they would set an example for the other tribes. A day was set for the rebellion to start and on the appointed day, the Carnutes slaughtered all the Roman citizens who had settled in the capital, Cenabum (Orleans). Cotuatus and Conconnetodumnus, the Carnute chieftains, had organised the massacre. Roman traders, dealers and businessmen were killed and thrown into the Loire. More serious for Caesar was that Caius Fufius Cita, in charge of grain supply for the legions, was one of the victims.

The news spread throughout all Gaul. Vercingetorix, the son of the great Arverni chief Celtillos, played an important role in getting the revolt to spread as far as possible. He harangued his clients, but the Arverni nobility including his uncle chased him out of Gergovia, considering his undertaking too hazardous. Vercingetorix did not renounce for all that. He travelled across the countryside, recruiting partisans among the humble. With his gang, he managed to return to Gergovia and oust his adversaries. Soon the crowd was proclaiming him king. Vercingetorix then sent messengers to the tribes all over Gaul to warn them that the Arverni were taking up arms. Most of the Gallic peoples joined him and entrusted him with supreme command of the insurrection. Alone the Aedui and the Rhemi remained faithful to Rome. Vercingetorix launched a first offensive, sent the Cadurci's chief, Lucterios, to the Ruteni, the Gabali and the Nitiobroges, and then with them launched

the invasion of the Roman province of Transalpine Gaul.

In a few weeks Vercingetorix, a name meaning "great warrior king", had appeared from nowhere and placed himself at the head of a general uprising of an unprecedented size. Vercingetorix had probably served earlier in the Gallic cavalry contingents used as auxiliaries by the Romans, but his name was not at all known. This sudden "rise to power" was surprising. It can be explained only by the prestigious past of his father Celtillos, by the military reputation of the Arverni, and also by Vercingetorix's personal charisma.

It was now however, at the head of 10 000 cavalry and four to five times as many infantry, that Vercingetorix got ready to defy Caesar. The Proconsul recruited twenty cohorts in Cisalpine and Transalpine Gaul which then became the Vth and VIth Legions, so that he could regain control of the province. Faced with his adversary's agile manoeuvring, Caesar took advantage of his own capacity for rapid action. After putting the Roman province on alert from Narbo, he rushed directly into Arverni territory. Right in the middle of winter, he crossed the snow-covered hills of the Vivarais, going through Helvii territory. Although the new recruits were worn out, he began systematically plundering Arverni territory. Vercingetorix was forced to hurry back defend his own lands. Caesar kept the initiative. He went to Vienne and rushing through Aedui territory, reached the two legions that were wintering with the

Lingones and which he was going to use as an escort. This was end of February, beginning of March. Caesar then joined up with the main part of his army and started campaigning in earnest. He had just managed to turn the situation around, mainly in his favour.

CENABUM, AVARICUM AND GERGOVIA

A struggle to the bitter end now started. Caesar's objective was now Cenabum, where the insurrection started. Vercingetorix was in the middle of besieging an oppidum belonging to the Boii, allies of the Aedui. The proconsul moved very quickly. He took Vellaunodunum in Senones territory then reached Cenabum, which he ruthlessly pillaged before burning it down. He had now avenged the besieged Roman citizens. Caesar then crossed the Liger (Loire) and marched towards Bituriges territory. He was clearly aiming for their capital Avaricum (Bourges).

Vercingetorix was caught unawares. He had given up his operations against the Boii to come and try out his new tactics on Caesar in Bituriges territory: he refused all contact and tried to attack the Roman army's supply sources. The young Arverni chieftain used a "scorched earth" policy forcing the legionaries to wander further away from the path they were advancing along to find supplies. The Gauls' cavalry attacked the isolated columns of Roman foragers, causing heavy losses. But the siege of Avaricum triggered off a dispute among the insurrectionists. The Bituriges, one of the most powerful tribes, didn't see why they should sacrifice their capital to the indirect strategy recommended by Vercingetorix. For fear of seeing themselves confronted with the same dilemma, other tribes supported the Bituriges'

demand. Avaricum was such a rich city with such high ramparts that Vercingetorix, for all his strategic perspicacity, finished by yielding and agreed to send troops to defend the oppidum. So when Caesar arrived with his legions, he had to deploy all his army's knowledge of siege warfare (*polieurce tique* [10]) to invest Avaricum. The siege was long and difficult. The Romans were not successful attacking Vercingetorix's army camp, established on too strong a position; they finally took 25 days, getting the town to fall in mid-April.

Avaricum was pillaged and the inhabitants killed. Only 800 combatants managed to escape and join Vercingetorix. The general enthusiasm accompanying the beginning of the rebellion had now considerably cooled.

After a few days' rest in the Bituriges capital which was brimming over with supplies, Caesar marched into Aedui territory to make it sure was still loyal. He went to Decetia (Decize) and settled the political rivalries among the Aedui in favour of Convictolitavis at Cotos' expense. By ensuring that the partisans of the alliance with Rome triumphed, the Proconsul thought the worst was over. Now that the Aedui had renewed their support for him, he could go back and attack Vercingetorix on his own territory. From a position of strength, Caesar was even able to afford to divide his force in two. He marched with six legions towards Gergovia telling his legate Labienus to go and put down the Senones and Parisii to the north, with four legions. But there was another change of heart among the Aedui putting Caesar in danger again. Indeed the 10 000 warriors being brought up by Convictolitavis to reinforce the Roman army let themselves be tempted by the Arverni's arguments and the money they promised the warriors if they joined the insurrection.

Caesar had to march to meet them, win them back over and get them to remain loyal to him. During his absence, the Roman camp in front of Gergovia was very badly attacked – a bad sign…. But Caesar was never as energetic as when he had his back to the wall. The Proconsul captured a hill near Gergovia and soon launched an attack to take control of another hill near the town, but part of his infantry, in no doubt about its own strength and carried away by the lure of booty, threw itself without thinking at the town. The lack of coordination and battle plan which characterised this unexpected attack, together with the energetic resistance by the town's defenders, resulted in a bloody failure for the Roman legionaries.

The rout which followed was only halted by the solid defensive position established by the Xth Legion. Once again Caesar's veterans saved things. But the Romans had nonetheless lost 700 men and especially 46 centurions who fought at the head of their

troops. It was the equivalent of less than two cohorts, or less than 2% of Caesar's forces, but the psychological effect was great on the Gauls who now saw in this success their first victory in a set battle. Prudently Caesar lifted the siege and went off to find Labienus more to the north and regroup all his army. The main consequence of the Battle of Gergo-

Eporedorix, the Aedui chieftain, calming his contemporaries' enthusiasm. (Illustration by H. de Nolhac, Private Coll.)

via was above all that the Aedui decided this time once and for all to defect and join Vercingetorix and the insurrection.

As for Labienus, he didn't waste any time either. He had just crossed the Seine heading northwards when the news from Gergovia reached him. Camulogenius with a large army of Gauls thought that victory was now changing sides. Caesar's legate moved along the opposite bank from his adversary to cut the Gauls off from their base at Agedincum. Labienus managed to cross back over the river and attacked the Gauls whom he beat decisively. Camulogenius moreover was killed in the fighting. Labienus reached Agedincum without encountering any further problems then joined up with Caesar in the Upper Seine region.

WHAT WERE VERCINGETORIX'S AND CAESAR'S INTENTIONS NOW?

Caesar had now regrouped his entire army. He had even reinforced it at the beginning of August, by recruiting German mercenary cavalry. None-

Gallic horseman. He is wearing the traditional pair of breeches. His tunic is covered with a leather garment and a coat of mail weighing about 22 lbs (10 kilos). The helmet is made of iron and fitted with wide cheek covers. His long sword is worn on the right hand side inside a long iron scabbard. It was light and only weighed a little more than a kilo. This armament was generally completed with a lance or one or several javelins which could be housed in a quiver hanging from the saddle. (Illustration by S. Baudouard)

S. BAUDOUARD

BRITANNIA

OCEANUS

GERMANIE
INFERIOR

BELGICA

GERMANIA
SUPERIOR

GALLIA ULTERIOR

OCEANUS

Lugdunum

AQUITANIA

PROVINCIA NARBONENSIS

HISPANIA

MARE INTERNUM

39

theless, ever since the Aedui had abandoned the Roman cause, almost all the Gallic tribes had joined the rebellion.

Rarely has a campaign ever given rise to so much controversy after the event as the one which was about to start. Some see an inspired trick on Caesar's part, leading Vercingetorix by the nose into the Alesia noose (Jérôme Carcopino); others see possible double dealing by Vercingetorix, to get rid of his Aedui rivals (Jacques Harmand); others see it as the most brilliant demonstration of the Celtic people's military values (Jean Markale). Vercingetorix's strategic talents were first magnified then maligned; Caesar's were generally recognised but submitted to the most diverging interpretations. It is therefore difficult to present a simple, undisputed account of the battle, all the more so as even the location of the battle itself is also open to question. It would seem however that Alesia is the product of two very clear strategies and the outcome sought by Caesar and Vercingetorix, both of whom were searching at that precise moment and for different reasons for a decisive event.

Vercingetorix's plan seemed quite clear cut. He wanted to resume his "scorched earth" policy and deprive the Romans of all supplies, thereby forcing them to leave Gaul. He also envisaged harassing them with his numerous cavalry which was theoretically the strong point of his army. Furthermore, taking advantage of the fact that Caesar's troops were then deployed in the northern third of Gaul, the Arverni chieftain launched his and his allies' warriors against the Roman province. The objectives were twofold: push the Gauls of the Provincia into abandoning Rome and forcing Caesar to quit "long-haired" Gaul.

As for Caesar, the motives for his move southwards, after his junction with Labienus are less clear. The Roman army at first headed through Lingones territory, one of the rare peoples still loyal to Caesar. It then marched towards the territory of the Sequani. There are several possible theories. The German historian, Göler, and the French Emperor, Napoleon III, in their writings, put forward the idea that the proconsul was marching towards Besançon to establish himself there, whence he could easily have gone to the assistance of the Roman province but also avoid giving the impression of leaving Gaul. For many others like Christian Goudineau, the objective of Julius Caesar's movement south was to return to the Provincia and help it as directly as possible. The main question lies in evaluating the situation of Caesar and his army were in. Was he at bay? Was he trying to get away as quickly as possible from the threat posed by Vercingetorix and his cavalry? Or on the contrary, was he manoeuvring to push Vercingetorix into making a mistake? According to André Berthier the first hypothesis is the correct one: this would explain a Roman move towards Geneva, the gateway to the Roman province through Sequani territory.

For Hans Delbrück, Caesar needed a position where he could re-supply and protect the province, and still maintain a certain pressure on "long-haired" Gaul. For him, a move along the valley of the Saône, perhaps as far as its confluent with the River Doubs, seemed most logical. By remaining on the right bank of the Saône he could also threaten the Aedui and detach a few legions to bring back some of the Sequani and Helvetii to reason. Besides the Saône was navigable as far as Gray and seemed to be an excellent supply route, in touch directly with Caesar's rear bases. The other uncertainty lies in Vercingetorix's possible view point. Would he risk a pitched battle? Would he allow Caesar to leave independent Gaul and content himself with skirmishes?

The historian André Berthier, like indeed Hans Delbrück, is convinced that the young chief of the Gauls had very clearly understood that if he did not defeat the Romans decisively in battle this time while they were still in an awkward position, they would come back stronger the following year and conquer Gaul once and for all. Was Caesar aware that Vercingetorix was ready to give battle at all costs?

What was the best strategy for the Gauls? Fight the Romans in open country or else block them with an impregnable oppidum which would he would use to finish them off.

THE GREAT CAVALRY BATTLE

Caesar and his army started moving in the direction of the Provincia and its supply sources, heading southeast from Agedincum, at the beginning of July 52 BC. Vercingetorix and his army at first shadowed him without attempting any action. At that moment the proconsul had a total of about 70 000 men, an army made up of 12 legions, a few contingents of light infantry and especially recently recruited German cavalry mercenaries. Vercingetorix's troops amounted to some 80 000 infantry and 15 000 cavalry. Now that they outnumbered the Romans in cavalry the Gauls thought they would try their luck. They carefully planned to attack the marching legions by the book before they got away. By destroying their impedimenta [11], the Gauls would put the Roman army in a very precarious position. The nobles of all the tribes making up this cavalry swore solemnly, on pain of disgrace, to pass through the Roman ranks twice. The battle

probably took place between the 9 and 18 July 52 BC. The Gauls formed up in three cavalry groups, two on the flanks and one blocking the head of the Roman column. The infantry stood by, ready to finish off their mounted troops' likely victory.

The Gallic cavalry now rushed at the marching column but the Roman legionaries halted, formed up into a square and defended their baggage, driving off the Gauls' repeated attacks. Caesar's German cavalry led the counter-attack and ended up hewing down the Gauls who were faithful to their oath and lost a lot of men; three of the most prestigious Aedui nobles, Cotos, Cavarillos and Eporedorix were even captured. The Gauls had failed because of Caesar's tactical mastery, constantly using the cavalry to act in support of the infantry and vice-versa, unlike Vercingetorix who never engaged his infantrymen, preferring to keep them at a distance, quite outside the battle. Finally the German cavalry clearly showed their superiority in combat over that of the Gauls. This victory evidently gave Caesar a psychological advantage and caused some doubt among the Gauls: they had lost their most celebrated fighters. The defeat was indeed complete and the losses huge.

Vercingetorix had to respond with the only arm remaining to him: his infantry. In order to keep Caesar in Gaul and possibly beat him, he needed a redoubtable refuge which would spare him the fate of the Helvetii or the Belgians, beaten in open country, and which would leave him with a chance of defeating the Romans once and for all. He therefore moved to Alesia, the Mandubii's oppidum.

THE SIEGE AND THE BATTLES OF ALESIA

The oppidum at Alesia was not chosen by chance. Supposed to be impregnable, the Mandubii's town indeed seemed to be just that, unlike Avaricum for instance, which is why Caesar never tried storming it; he was quite content just to blockade it. Alesia is also described as being the site of one of the most important religious sanctuaries in Gaul: this is another interesting criterion as to why the place was chosen: resisting there would be understood by all the Gallic peoples. Did Vercingetorix or Caesar actually think beforehand about this, that this oppidum would be where the final battle was to be fought? It is probable that the former prepared the position in advance in case his cavalry was defeated. Caesar manoeuvring and forcing Vercingetorix to fight the battle so that the Gauls would then go and shut themselves up inside Alesia seems to be too tenuous a view point to defend. Whatever the reason, Vercingetorix went to Alesia because he knew that Caesar would follow him there. We are now probably in the last week of July.

AFTER HIS CAVALRY WAS DEFEATED, Vercingetorix at once sent his infantry towards Alesia, the oppidum refuge which he had planned in advance would save him. The Gallic chieftain did not go back through his camp and had his baggage train moved to the oppidum by another route. This caught Caesar, whose pursuit has stopped with nightfall after taking 3 000 Gauls prisoner, off balance.

RENDEZVOUS AT ALESIA

After his cavalry was defeated, Vercingetorix at once sent his infantry towards Alesia, the oppidum refuge which he had planned in advance would save him. The Gallic chieftain did not go back through his camp and had his baggage train moved to the oppidum by another route. This caught Caesar, whose pursuit has stopped with nightfall after taking 3 000 Gauls prisoner, off balance.

In one great leg, the Gauls reached Alesia. Vercingetorix set up a camp there with makeshift entrenchments at the foot of the oppidum walls, facing the great plain which his army had just come across. The idea was no doubt to keep a base outside the

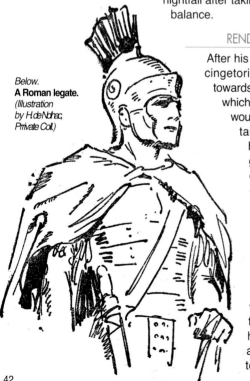

oppidum. Sheltered by the oppidum, the camp would enable the Arverni chieftain to launch operations to harass Caesar and prevent him from investing the place. Vercingetorix also ordered a wall (maceria) to be built, as forward protection for this same camp. Caesar summarised these enemy dispositions with great clarity: *"at the foot of the rampart, all the eastern flank of the hill was occupied by the Gallic troops and in front they had dug a ditch and built a crude six-foot high wall."* [12]

What Vercingetorix thought of doing was repeating the strategy which he had used successfully at Gergovia: establish his army in a solid defensive position, thwart the Romans by preventing them from totally blockading the place, carry out targeted counter-attacks, and force the enemy to admit failure and lift the siege. To get ready for the difficult battle ahead, Vercingetorix had his supplies brought to Alesia in advance. Despite his cavalry's defeat, the Gallic chieftain still had faith in his men and in his strategy. He kept all his soldiers with him including the cavalry defeated the day before. This choice suggests that Vercingetorix was thinking of going over to the attack as soon as he could, and that he would not be just satisfied with a "garrison" to defend the walls of Alesia.

Caesar reached Alesia shortly after the Gauls. He immediately spread out his legions around the oppidum. The proconsul ordered the usual camps to be built, but also a string of little forts (23 in all) positioned, in his own words, in "the right places", and the investment of the Alesia stronghold to be organised. His objective was not to assault the place, like Gergovia, but to besiege it according to the book. The big

camps were there for the legions, to give them a solid base. The little forts were intended for small mobile garrisons to prevent the Gauls from making sorties both by night and by day, and at the same time to protect the Roman contingents who were building other, vaster earthworks.

Very quickly it appeared that the great plain situated "in front of the oppidum" (ante oppidum, to quote Caesar's terms), was going to be the focal point of the fighting. The proconsul described it as 3 000 paces long and because of its area, it was of course the weak point of the Roman investment work. It was also the only place where the Gauls could deploy counter-attacks en masse, since the oppidum's other slopes were bordered by two streams and precipices.

Caesar used the terms flumina and praerupta to describe them, which corresponds to the description used for large military obstacles. Watching Caesar's legionaries working, Vercingetorix soon had to face up to the reality of the situation.

The extent of the investment work carried out by the Romans was showing him that what he had though impossible – a total blockade of Alesia – was on the contrary actually happening. At that precise moment, Vercingetorix was still in a position to react and regain the initiative.

ANOTHER CAVALRY FIGHT

In the initial phase the Romans worked, concentrating on the plain. It was where Vercingetorix would logically choose to launch his first counter-attack to thwart all the Alesia investment work done by Caesar. The Gallic cavalry therefore sallied forth from the camp situated at the foot of the oppidum and fell upon the Roman legionaries hard-at-work. Caesar had obviously not left his men without protection. The Roman cavalry was billeted nearby and intervened immediately to drive back the enemy cavalry. Caesar speaks of *"extreme ferocity on both sides"*, which was hardly surprising. In all the fighting during the wars against the Gauls, the Roman cavalry never managed to defeat the Gallic cavalry without the help of other Gauls or more recently the Germans. These new confrontations were no exception to the rule and *"Caesar sent the Germans to the aid of our flagging men and placed the legions in front of the camp to prevent the enemy infantry from suddenly attacking."*[13] The manoeuvre was crystal clear and was a copy of the successful cavalry battle won a few days earlier. The German cavalry intervened as the strike force which would prove decisive, the legions advanced as the second line in support of the cavalry. As with their previous defeat, the Gallic cavalry was suddenly all isolated because Vercingetorix, unlike Caesar, definitely didn't want to risk his infantry in a pitched battle. It seems that the Germans launched their attack on the northern flank of the Gauls, along the foot of the hill situated to the north, and struck out of the blue. The Gauls who did not have the necessary reserves to protect themselves were taken by surprise. The cavalry fell back in great disorder towards the narrow gates of the camp where their numbers created a bottleneck; the throng became indescribable, all the more so as the Germans, whose horses were still fresh, pursued the Gauls keenly. They started butchering Vercingetorix's cavalry stalled outside the camp. The Gallic infantry guarding the camp also started to panic and sounded the alert.

A lot of cavalrymen abandoned their mounts and tried to climb over the palisades and get into the oppidum. Vercingetorix now understood that his troops were on the verge of catastrophe. He had to take energetic action. To prevent the defeated cavalry now filling the camp from getting into the oppidum which was a much better refuge, he had all the gates of Alesia closed. Now with no way out, the infantry garrisoning the camp stood and fought sufficiently steadfastly for Caesar to call it a day. He ordered his catapults to fire a few shots and cause a bit more disorder among the Gauls, but at the same time also ordered the Germans to fall back; they obeyed bringing a large number of the horses the Gauls had abandoned outside the camp back with them. It was only then that the Roman legio-

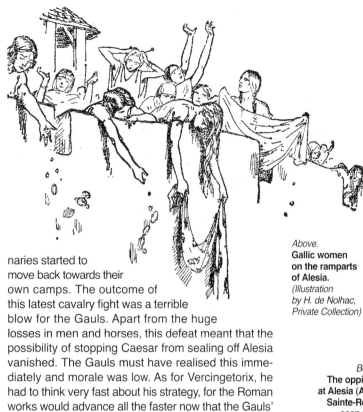

naries started to move back towards their own camps. The outcome of this latest cavalry fight was a terrible blow for the Gauls. Apart from the huge losses in men and horses, this defeat meant that the possibility of stopping Caesar from sealing off Alesia vanished. The Gauls must have realised this immediately and morale was low. As for Vercingetorix, he had to think very fast about his strategy, for the Roman works would advance all the faster now that the Gauls' cavalry was no longer a threat.

Should the Gauls' chieftain have left leave Alesia,

Above.
**Gallic women
on the ramparts
of Alesia.**
*(Illustration
by H. de Nolhac,
Private Collection)*

Below.
**The oppidum
at Alesia (Alise-
Sainte-Reine)
seen from
the south-south-east.**
(Private Collection, RR)

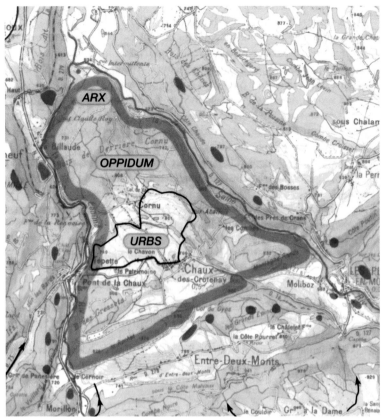

raging for several centuries as to how many combatants Vercingetorix kept with him in Alesia, once he had sent his cavalry back to their respective tribes to rally support. There is no debate about the Roman forces present, except for the exact strength of the two legions levied in 52 BC and that of the German cavalry which are both still only approximate. An estimation of an army of 70 000 combatants, roughly the same as during the cavalry battle, is therefore very likely. The numbers that Vercingetorix kept with him inside Alesia are uncertain. They must be between Caesar's estimate of 80 000 men and the 20 000 men according to the German historian Delbrück, who suggests that logically Vercingetorix only kept the elite of his army (20 000 out of maybe 80 000) inside the stronghold since they would be ample to defend it. Economising mouths to feed would probably also enable the besieged to hold out longer. This confirms how powerful the oppidum actually was and how inevitable the siege became.

Others did not fail to draw attention to the fact that *"if there were not more than 20 000 men in the oppidum, how could Caesar have given his 70 000 legionaries one prisoner each? For it was in the oppidum that he took prisoners and it can be gleaned from the text (Book VII, 88) that the captured Gauls from the relief army were later massacred. And if he didn't, how is it that no one made a note of the many disappointed senior officers who would surely have protested and who took Pompey's side a short time later (Labienus) or would be among the conspirators in 44 BC (the young Decimus Brutus, not to be confused with Caesar's assassin, Marcus Junius Brutus, or Trebonius."* [14]

The strength of the relieving army which soon appeared before the walls of Alesia is even harder to estimate. Caesar mentions 240 000 men and Delbrück 60 000; other historians give figures somewhere in the middle, around 100 000 men. The fact that there were about 8 000 cavalry among them constitutes a rather reliable guide. The lower or middle estimates seem to conform to the rea-

should he have kept all his army with him if he chose to stay put? Finally, a few days later and in the middle of the night, Vercingetorix decided to send his last cavalry away; their job was to avoid the Romans and return thirty days later (a period equivalent to his own grain reserves), with reinforcements levied from all over Gaul. He chose to remain in person in Alesia, even if it meant getting cornered among the network of fortifications which the Romans were in the process of putting up. It was clear to him that Alesia was going to be the last battle, the one which would decide the outcome of the war. It was no longer a question of shilly-shallying or abandoning the oppidum to its fate, as was the case with Avaricum. It was at Alesia that Vercingetorix decided to win or die. He now had a clear idea of what his plan was going to be: he was going to rely on mobilising all the rebelling tribes and put his fate into the hands of the formidable relief army he hoped he'd be able to assemble to help him: it would be the hammer, and the oppidum and its garrison at Alesia would be the anvil.

HOW MANY MEN WERE PRESENT AT ALESIA?

An intense debate has been

CÉSAR VISITANT LES TRAVAUX

Roman legionary and centurion on one of the Alesia fortification towers. Built at regular intervals along the circumvallation and the counter-vallation which securely surrounded the Gallic oppidum, the towers enabled them to observe the movements of the besieged and the rescue army. From their platforms, the Romans could also shoot arrows at the Gauls.
(Illustration by S. Baudouard)

Above.
**Reconstitution
of what the Roman
camp may have
looked like.**
(Private Collection, DR)

Below.
**Cut-away
of the Gauls'
fortifications at Alesia.**
*(Atlas belongin
to Napoleon III,
Private Collection)*

lity of the period: in the France of his time which had a bigger population, when conscription was already quite well organised, Napoleon could never manage to levy more than 100 000 men within 30 days.

On the other hand in the Gaul of the period, all men were prospective warriors and could quickly be enrolled for fighting. It's more the question of logistics and supplies which pose problems and raise questions. There are some objections however to the assumptions about the numbers Caesar gave. They are based mainly on the fact that, unless they really did greatly

outnumber the enemy, the Gauls would probably never have dared to attack the Romans as they were able to do, several days in a row and in several places on the battlefield. Be that as it may, even before the relief army arrived, Caesar was already in great danger. Brought to a halt in hostile territory, in the middle of a Gaul whose tribes were virtually all up in arms against Roman might, the proconsul and his army could not show even the slightest sign of weakness.

ALESIA SEALED OFF

The situation the Romans were in would explain the considerable effort the legionaries made to render their position more secure. They gradually built up a double ring of fortifications, protecting it with ditches, flooded in the lowest parts, and a whole system of the most varied array of traps. Vercingetorix no doubt underestimated the rapidity and the extent of Caesar's work. Indeed the Roman chief's plan most likely surpassed what even his adversaries had imagined was possible. Caesar was warned by deserters that the Gallic tribes were mobilising with the intention of gathering together a huge reinforcement army and had to take the appropriate defensive measures to meet this threat. Neither could he relax his efforts in keeping up the siege of Vercingetorix's troops inside Alesia.

The proconsul logically brought his attention to bear on the oppidum intending to cut it off from all outside contact. He therefore had a first network of trenches, called the contrevallum, dug in order to seal the place off. Did these fortifications form a continuous line

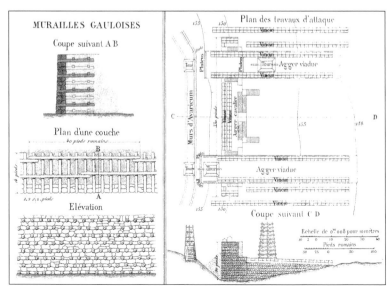

of ditches, embankments, palisades and towers? It's not very likely. Using the 23 little forts built as his base in the early days of the siege together with the legion's camps, Caesar completed his disposition with special defences, adapting their size and form to the lie of the land. Obviously in the plain he deployed most of the means needed to render an attack by the Gauls well nigh impossible.

He had a deep ditch dug with steep, vertical sides to block the plain and slow down any approach made by the besieged Gauls; then little 12-inch wooden spikes tipped with small metal needles (stimuli) were placed about 15 yards further back; then he had a large number of "wolf's holes" dug in the shape of three-feet deep cones (lis or lilia) with a fire-hardened wooden spike (stipite) planted at the bottom of each one; then came the cippi (bark-less trees and branches tied together); behind these, two further parallel ditches and finally the embankment on which were built the wooden ramparts also protected by sharpened branches (cervi). Towers with firing platforms were installed at regular intervals, about 25 yards apart so that projectiles could be thrown down onto the attackers. Once this contravallum was finished, Caesar carried out similar "works" (his own words), but this time turned "outwards".

These defensive works comprised a circumvallation intended to protect the Roman troops when the relief army arrived in their rear. Caesar said that the total perimeter ran to more than 12 ½ miles, which most likely means that the fortifications must have been determined by the natural difficulties of the terrain itself. Caesar had planned for his troops to be able to move around very quickly between the two lines of fortifications from one point of the besieged

oppidum to another. There were six legionaries' camps in the plain, each housing one or two legions, maybe three. They were also situated between the two rings, except one camp for two legions positioned on a hill north of Alesia. This camp was also protected by ditches and traps but remained nonetheless outside the circumvallation. Caesar set up his headquarters in the great camp on the plain. In order to finish these works, the Romans were assigned to do different tasks simultaneously like defending the position, fetching materials, building the works and getting supplies in. The Gauls tried several times to sally forth in different directions to take advantage of the reduced numbers of legionaries under arms. These threats only served to strengthen Caesar's resolve even further and reinfor-

Above.
Vestiges of a Roman installation. There were parts of the Romans' "temporary" forts which were in fact permanent installations.
(DR)

Below.
Model of a section of the fortifications and the traps set up by the Romans around Alesia.
(© Archéodrome, Private Collection)

ROMAN SIDE   **GALLIC SIDE**

ce the fortifications all the more, especially by inventing new "traps" likely to cool the enemy's fervour. The Roman leader had clearly understood that the besieged, from their central position, could attack him simultaneously at several different points. Caesar's objective was therefore to slow their attacks down as much as possible with the ditches and traps and give his cohorts the time to assemble and reinforce the threatened places.

As the Roman fortifications got more and more imposing, Vercingetorix and the besieged troops started getting worried, even demoralised. After thirty days' waiting the relieving army was still not in sight and supplies were beginning to run out. During a council of war, voices were raised, envisaging negotiations or even surrender. Others wanted to try a general sally even though this solution offered practically no chance of success. In his account, Caesar speaks of one Critognatos, an Arvernii aristocrat, who had tried to persuade the assembly to wait at all costs for the relief army since only a concerted attack from both sides could bring victory. The council finally decided that this was the wisest course of action and chose to reduce the number of mouths that needed feeding in the besieged town by expelling the Mandubii civilians still present in Alesia.

The women, children and old men were therefore sent to the Roman contravallation. Caesar refused to meet them or even to let them through. No doubt he didn't have anything to give them in the way of food, but he also feared the chaos they would cause if they passed through the camps. By leaving them to die of hunger between the contravallation and the oppidum, the proconsul carried on with his psychological war, aimed at further sapping the Gauls' morale. As for them, they did not go back on their initial decision, either and did not let the Mandubii come back into the oppidum. The die was now cast and the besieged Gauls' supply problems did not give their leaders any

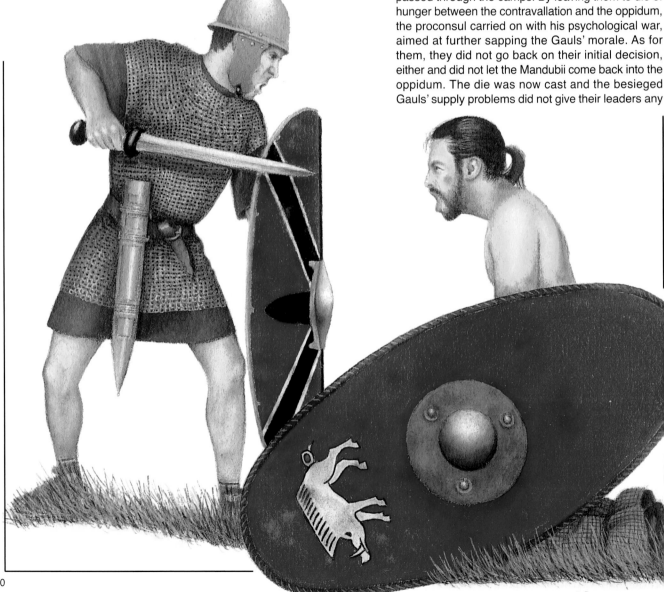

S. BAUDOUARD

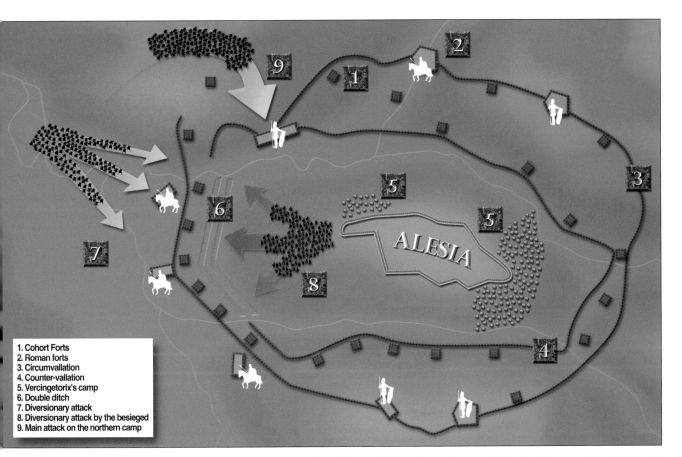

1. Cohort Forts
2. Roman forts
3. Circumvallation
4. Counter-vallation
5. Vercingetorix's camp
6. Double ditch
7. Diversionary attack
8. Diversionary attack by the besieged
9. Main attack on the northern camp

ALESIA

© Pascal Da Silva, 2011

real margin for action. It is interesting to note that Caesar does not mention Vercingetorix's attitude during all this period. The young war lord seemed strangely silent, leaving the most important role to Critognatos and not speaking during the council of war. He does not seem to have intervened in the discussions concerning the Mandubii's expulsion. Was his position as supreme chieftain weakened by the dramatic turn of events? Did Vercingetorix remain apart in order to better prepare the forthcoming battle? All during 52 BC and at Avaricum in particular, Vercingetorix weighed heavily in the war councils in order to impose his opinions. A few days before the supreme combat, his detached position seems strange. Maybe it was only the reflection of what Caesar wanted to show in his account of the war against the Gauls.

THE REINFORCEMENT ARMY

The outcome of the battle now depended on the reinforcements arriving, on their numbers and their worth in battle. The reinforcements which Gaul had decided to send to Vercingetorix's rescue assembled in Aedui territory. A war council met in order to fix the numbers that each tribe had to supply and to choose the army leaders. A purely "massed levy", as Vercingetorix no doubt would have wanted, was rejected

out of hand. It would have been impossible to feed this uncontrollable mass of soldiers resulting from this general mobilisation and shift it to Alesia. Estimated numbers have therefore been determined for each of the big tribes or great regions of independent Gaul.

Only the Bellovacii, who asserted that they wanted to

TABLE OF THE ESTIMATED STRENGTH OF THE REINFORCEMENT ARMY (ACCORDING TO CAESAR)[15]

PEOPLES	ESTIMATED CONTINGENT	PEOPLES	ESTIMATED CONTINGENT
Aedui and their clients *(the Segustiani, Ambivariti, Aulerci, Brannovices and Blanovii)*	35 000	**Ambiani**	5 000
		Mediomatricii	5 000
		Petrocorii	5 000
Arvernii and their clients *(the Euletetes, Cadurcii, Gabali and Vellavi)*	35 000	**Nervii**	5 000
		Morini	5 000
Sequani	12 000	**Nitiobroges**	5 000
Senones	12 000	**Aulerci Cénomani**	5 000
Bituriges	12 000	**Atrébates**	4 000
Santones	12 000	**Véliocasses**	3 000
Ruteni	12 000	**Lexobii**	3 000
Carnutes	12 000	**Aulerci Eburovices**	3 000
Bellovaci	10 000	**Raurarci**	1 000
Pictones	8 000	**Boïi**	1 000
Turones	8 000	**Coriosolites**	20 000
Parisii	8 000	**Redones, Ambibarri, Caletes, Osismes,**	
Helvetii	8 000	**Lemovices, Unelles.**	

wage war against Caesar for their own ends, refused to submit to the council's decisions. They accepted to supply a symbolic 2 000 men so that they wouldn't be considered as traitors. The tribes who had already been bled to death in the earlier campaigns, like the Nervii, sent fewer men than the Arvernii or the Aedui who made up the biggest contingents in the reinforcement army.

The uncertainties concerning the strength of the relieving army have already been mentioned and the weakness of its cavalry seems to have been attested. There were only 8 000 cavalry in its ranks. The names of the leading chieftains are more certain. At the head, the council gave joint com-

mand to four men. These were Vercassivellaunos, an Arverni, who belonged to Vercingetorix's family. He represented a sort of pledge of loyalty towards his cousin, now cornered in Alesia. There were also two Aedui Viridomaros and Eporedorix which confirmed the important role Rome's former ally had now taken in the uprising against Caesar.

Finally the fourth chief was an Atrebates, Comnios. He had served for a long time as a faithful auxiliary with Caesar. He was now one of the leading chieftains in Gaul, recognised for his qualities as a tactician and his worth in combat. He had the advantage of knowing the Roman army well, a very useful point when hoping to defeat it.

It was about a week beyond the 30 days' limit that the relief army finally got there, somewhere between 25 August and 3 September 52 BC. The soldiers set up their camp on a hill, a mile from Alesia. The besieged army had now run out of supplies so the newcomers would have to act fast. At once. It was probably for this reason that the chieftains started another cavalry battle on the day following their arrival without much thought for tactics.

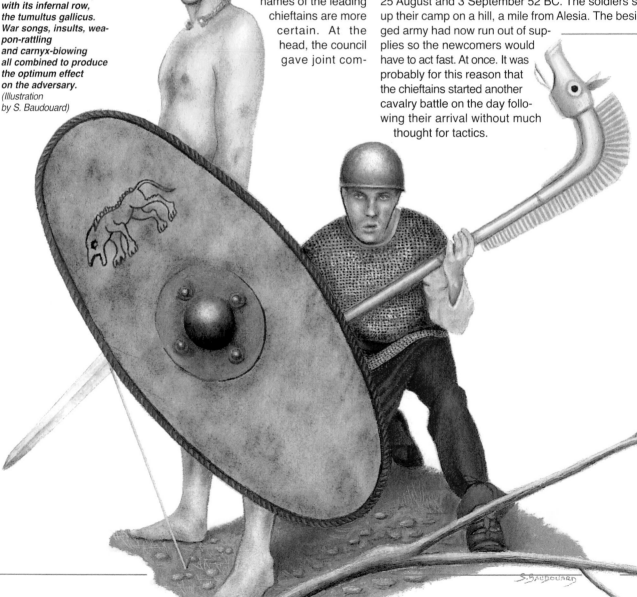

Carnute warrior and carnyx-player. This 5' 6" (1.70 m) bronze trumpet was surmounted with a boar's head. It had a potent sound and was intended to astound the enemy with its infernal row, the tumultus gallicus. War songs, insults, weapon-rattling and carnyx-biowing all combined to produce the optimum effect on the adversary.
(Illustration by S. Baudouard)

THE FIGHTING ON THE FIRST AND SECOND DAYS

The second phase of the battle of Alesia started therefore just like the first one had finished, with a clash between opposing cavalry. The reasons which pushed the Gauls into launching their cavalry against the Romans on the plain from the outset are not easy to establish. What was certain was that it was not this cavalry which would be able to break through the circumvallation and then relieve Alesia.

THERE WERE SEVERAL FACTORS which might have justified engaging the cavalry immediately. It was possible that the relieving army chiefs wanted to prove how war-like they were to Vercingetorix, by fighting immediately while the infantry got ready for more massive assaults. It was also probable that among the relief army's cavalry there were many who had been among those beaten beneath the walls of the oppidum and then sent away to get help.

These mounted troops, reputed to be the best warriors in the army, would want revenge. One must therefore see in this attack a sort of challenge. Besides, Caesar moving his cavalry out of the camps, when there was no other reason for doing so, seemed to confirm this idea.

With the Gauls deploying their cavalry across the two-mile wide plain in front of the oppidum, Caesar launched his cavalry to meet it, with foot auxiliaries accompanying it. The Gallic cavalry was also escorted by voltigeurs and archers. It was the first time that Celtic cavalry was to be seen fighting like this, with tactical support from foot soldiers.

The influence of Comnios who was used to Roman tactics can perhaps be seen here. The infantry in the reinforcement army deployed on the neighbouring heights and the Gauls inside Alesia, climbing up onto the ramparts, rejoiced at the start of the decisive fighting and tried to see the plain and watch the outcome. As with the battle the previous month, the fighting was very fierce.

Charge followed charge all afternoon. The battle lasted indeed from midday to sundown, i.e. around 7 pm at that time of year. The Gallic cavalry was not undeserving and their foot soldiers caused casualties among the Roman squadrons when they launched their counter-attacks. Neither side won a decisive advantage until the end of the day when Caesar launched his redoubtable German cavalry again, for a combined attack. Once again their action forced the decision. At the sight of them the Gauls panicked just at the place the German mercenaries were concentrating all their effort. This panic spread to the whole relief army cavalry. The Gauls were totally outclassed by the German cavalry and now had to fall back in disorder. After so any hours of indecisive fighting, the Gauls were nonetheless very disappointed. But no dejection was to be seen anywhere. The four reinforcement army chiefs immediately got together. They decided for a night-time attack against the fortifications in the plain, hoping thus to take advantage of surprise protected by the darkness.

Below.
Roman legionaries going into the attack against the walls, eagerly defended by Vercingetorix's Gauls.
(Illustration by H. de Nolhac, Private Collection)

After their defeat, the Gauls returned to their camps for the night and spent all the following day making assault equipment: screens, ladders for crossing obstacles and traps, siege hooks for trying to tear the palisades off the ramparts. They had also to think up another plan. One of the Gauls' main problems was coordinating the attacks between the relieving army outside and those inside Alesia. From where the troops had installed their camp, it was most probable that the new attack would be directed against the fortifications on the plain, the easiest ones for the relief army to get to. Vercingetorix could only watch and guess what his would-be rescuers' intentions were. He had units ready to intervene at any moment. The relief army chiefs had been able to observe in detail all the Roman fortifications and the positions of the legions' camps. They understood that between his two rings of trenches, Caesar could move his cohorts about very easily and concentrate his troops at any points under threat.

Rescue could only come with the use of surprise and a quick assault. It had to be a massive attack allowing the enemy no time to find out quickly enough where the relief army was making the main attack.

The war council rapidly opted for a night attack so that the men would be able to approach the circumvallation without being seen. To make things easier, the place chosen for the attack was again the plain where it was easier to concentrate large units. The attack was to be launched in the middle of the night. As soon as it was dark enough, the Gauls slowly closed in on the circumvallation on the plain in utmost silence. Lying on the ground, the combatants waited for all the troops to be in position before going over to

Above.
Example of fortified walls erected by the Romans.
(DR)

Below.
Gallic archers given the task of defending the walls of the town of Alesia.
(Illustration by H. de Nolhac, Private Collection)

the attack. The attackers suddenly uttered terrible shouts and started to attack. The point of shouting at just the moment of the attack was as much to frighten the Romans as to warn Vercingetorix that he could to attack at the same place and break through the vice which was strangling him.

Although the night gave the attackers an advantage by obliging the Romans to fire their arbalests without aiming, it did not make their task any easier when they tried to avoid the zone where the traps had been set, in front of the circumvallation. Before reaching it, the Gauls – there were a lot of them - had succeeded in alarming the Roman defence by the density of their projectiles. Archers and slingers did their best to aim at the palisades where the legionaries had started to appear. Once within the perimeter covered with traps, the Gauls' progression slowed right down. Despites the screens thrown to cover the obstacles, there were lots of warriors who got caught in the stimuli or fell into the lilia. On his side Vercingetorix put himself at the head of his warriors but his men got caught up in the large ditch dug a long way from the circumvallation, without even being able to fight.

The fighting rapidly intensified on the side of the relieving army; it was mainly fighting in which the protagonists on both sides fired arrows, stones, and javelins blindly into the night and eventually the big arrows and stones from the Roman artillery which despite the dark turned out to be very deadly. The Romans in the shelter of their ramparts and from up on their towers, were both better protected and better placed to fire.

Their position was nonetheless difficult to hold as the Gauls got closer. The Roman army was lucky in that it had solid and experienced leaders. That night, the plains sector was entrusted to legates M. Antonius and C. Trebonius, who had several campaigns to their credit already. They therefore reacted calmly to the situation, so much so that Caesar paid tribute to them and mentioned them in his account of the battle: *"the darkness prevented us seeing in front and the losses were heavy on both sides. The ballistae launched a rain of bolts. Moreover the legates, M. Antonius and C. Trebonius, who were in charge of this sector, sent reinforcements taken from the little forts situated in the rear to the points where they understood we were showing signs of weakening."* [16]

As Caesar's troops handled things with their per-fect organisation and their leaders' mastery, the Gauls showed how inexperienced they were in such matters. The besieged troops wasted precious time bringing up materiel for filling in the steep-sided ditch or crossing it, so much so, that when day started breaking, they had not even got over the obstacle. At the same time the relieving army soldiers had not even been able to break through the circumvallation anywhere. Caught up in and slowed down by the traps, and

Roman legate and Gallic auxiliary horseman in Roman service. The horseman is wearing an extra garment over his coat of mail which protected his torso and shielded his cuirass from the sun better. Indeed wearing a coat of mail in the sun became unbearable very quickly. The legate was the officer commanding the legion. In Caesar's day the legate was chosen for his competence, relegating the tribunes – young aristocrats in search of the titles they needed for political advancement – to purely honorary roles.
(Illustration by S. Baudouard)

Above.
Cutaway map of the Roman fortifications in front of Alesia. This view has been interpreted by Peter Conolly, the English specialist of war in the Graeco-Roman period.
(Illustration by Peter Conolly, RR, Private Collection))

stopped by the ditches, the Gauls were never able to get close enough to the Romans to fight them hand to hand.

At first light it was the threat of a Roman sally against their right flank that persuaded the relief army chiefs to give up the assault. Seeing his brothers in arms retreat, Vercingetorix was also forced to back off. The Gauls returned to their camps and the oppidum with the same sense of discouragement. There were several lessons to be learnt from the failure of the night attack. The Gauls had found out how deep and strong the Roman entrenchments were, how well they were organised, how capable they were of rapidly mobilising reinforcements; and how important it was to be more coordinated with Vercingetorix's troops, who had not been able to fight during the night because they had not got into position fast enough to join in the relief army's attack.

A NEW BATTLE PLAN

The reinforcement army chiefs had twice concentrated their efforts on the plains sector, only two miles wide. The Romans would have been at a bit of a loss had they had to disperse their forces around Alesia: the Gauls had made their task easier by attacking a single point, both from outside and inside. The steep nature of the terrain mentioned by Caesar in his Bellum Gallicum could explain things, at least partly. The relieving army was large and it would not have been easy to move it round the circumvallation along narrow or perilous tracks. There was also another important element; the relief army chieftains were not locals, they did not know the lie of the land well and in their haste chose to attack in the most easily accessible sector.

After two bloody failures, things were bound to change. The war council met again and everybody agreed that a new, more "subtle" plan had to be thought out. The chiefs took the time to listen to the locals who described all the Roman fortifications with their strong and weak points to them. They also sent men out to reconnoitre and confirm what had been said. From these "consultations" and these "explorations", it turned out that the camp for the two legions, set up lower down on the hill situated to the north of Alesia, was particularly exposed. It was linked to the circumvallation but the entrenchments could actually be attacked from the heights.

The main camp itself had the same disadvantage which was why Caesar had billeted two veteran legions, probably the Xth under by Caius Caninius, and the XIth led by Antistius Reginus. The Gauls therefore decided to attack the north camp with their best troops. For safety's sake, it was also decided, and for the first time, to make a simultaneous attack in order to trick the Romans as to the direction of the main attack. It was once again on the plain that this diversionary attack was to take place.

As with the night attack, the relief army chiefs relied on Vercingetorix to take the Romans in the rear. During their first two sallies, the besieged Gauls had already sufficiently filled in the ditch not to waste time on their approach this third time. The fact that the Gauls limited themselves to two attacks in the north-west sector of Alesia tended to prove two points: they were not numerous enough to do more and the terrain of the other sectors was unsuitable for an attack in strength. Vercassivellaunos was given a manoeuvre which might almost have succeeded. He had to go round the northern mountain with the army's elite, especially the Arvernii. It was no doubt because he was Vercingetorix's cousin and an Arvernii like him that he was entrusted with this decisive mission. After spending the day getting ready, Vercassivellaunos made his night-time approach march, moving widely round the camp in order not to attract the Romans' attention.

He got into position at daybreak and made his men rest; there were perhaps 20 000 of them. The attack was planned for midday when the sun reached its zenith.

THE SUPREME COMBAT

When the shouting Gauls indicated that fighting had resumed, it was understood by both camps that this was the decisive fight. After several failures, Vercingetorix and the relief army chiefs this time had, once and for all, to overrun the Roman earthworks. As for Caesar, he knew that if he could hold fast, the Gauls would give up the fight.

It was during the attack on the Roman camp located on the other side of the north mountain, the weak point in the Roman lines, that the fighting was the fiercest. The Gallic troops taking part, the most experienced in the relief army, acted this time in an orderly and methodical manner. Vercassivellaunos took the precaution of having reserves always ready to take over from the exhausted attackers. His men brought earth in their coats to fill in the traps. In the first group the Gallic warriors took advantage of their dominant position to throw bolts of all sorts at the Romans. The soldiers in the second group did not rush pointlessly into the attack but rather attacked sheltering behind their shields. In a certain way they were imitating the Roman "tortoise" whose effectiveness they had already witnessed in other battles. Bit by bit the Romans started to give ground. Caesar, who from the outset of the fighting, had placed himself where he could survey the turn of events, did not fail to react. He at once sent his best lieutenant, Labienus to bring the situation back under control with six cohorts as reinforcements.

On the plain, the other relieving army chiefs had launched as many soldiers as possible into the attack to cover as wide a front as possible. But in that area, despite the damage done to the traps and the defences during the night attack the circumvallation, just like the contravallation, was still a formidable obstacle. In places the Gauls were a serious threat to the ramparts, but the Roman officers motivated their men who managed to drive off the attackers. Vercingetorix's soldiers were the fiercest in combat and for the first time they at last reached the contravallation without however being able to break through it. Caesar nonetheless had to go personally to the spot to exhort his troops. The number of attacks the Gauls made rendered his task all the more difficult.

The situation was now stabilised despite the strength of the Gauls' initial attacks, both against the northern camp and  in the plain. Vercingetorix also showed he had tactical good sense. Seeing that the situation was blocked and the contravallation impregnable in the sector of his first attack, he had his men fall back with all their materiel into Alesia before launching them into another attack down the south flank of the oppidum. The steep terrain there was more to his advantage and the Roman defences were less imposing. With the same causes having the same effects, this second attack was as successful as Vercassivellaunos'. The Gauls managed to reach the rampart palisades and tore them down with their hooks. They chased the Romans from the towers and were on the point of breaching the contravallation.

Once again the proconsul's expert glance prevented Vercingetorix from getting across that last obstacle. Seeing the situation going badly in this sou-

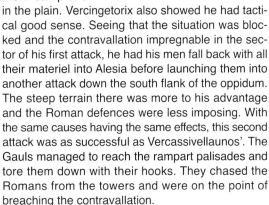

Above.
The oath taken by Gallic horsemen before their attempt to break through the Roman lines.
(Illustration by H. de Nolhac, Private Collection)

Below.
Reconstitution of a Roman watchtower, part of the fortifications surrounding the site at Alesia.
(DR)

thern sector, where he had not expected such a violent attack, Caesar sent reinforcements there on the double. Decimus Junius Brutus went into action with several fresh cohorts. Despite his efforts, Brutus was not able to check Vercingetorix's attack, forcing Caesar to send Caius Fabius Maximus with further reinforcements. The situation became more and more delicate. For the second time Caesar went to the spot in person, to the hottest place, with other cohorts in reinforcement and this time the attackers were driven off.

He did not have the time to savour the slightest moment of respite, for messengers from the northern camp which he could no longer see from where he now was, announced that Labienus was in great difficulty.

Despite the six cohorts sent to reinforce the twenty already present in the camp, Vercassivellaunos' Gauls were in the process of getting hold of the towers and the palisades. In great peril, Labienus had called in all the *garrisons from the neighbouring little forts: "Seeing that neither the earthworks nor the ditches were stopping the enemy's momentum, Labienus gathered together 39 cohorts, which he was lucky enough to be able to withdraw from neighbouring positions, and informed Caesar of what he believed he had to do."* [17]

The legate had managed to get hold of thirteen new cohorts. In the northern camp sector, Labienus was at the head of the equivalent of four legions. He was indeed in command of the same number of legions as a few months earlier during his campaign against Camulogenius. The legate now had to show that he was worthy of Caesar's trust. Labienus got ready to make another sally, as his leader had already authorised him to do. But the proconsul felt that

his personal intervention was going to be needed once again. Draped in his purple cloak (paludamentum), he led the last four available cohorts, assembled on his way towards the northern camp. At the same time he ordered half the cavalry to follow him between the circumvallation and the contravallation, and the other half to come out of its entrenchments and attack the Gauls in their rear.

The Gauls recognised Caesar and on his approach they went all out. Vercassivellaunos rushed to the assault and they threw themselves against Labienus' cohorts which had sallied from the camp to meet them. This time it was the moment of truth. The fighting was now sword against gladius and the maul was bloody.

Neither Labienus nor Vercassivellaunos seemed to be getting the upper hand, but when the squadrons of German cavalry all of a sudden turned up behind the Gauls, it made them break rank. Seized with panic the Gauls fled in disorder. Other reinforcements arrived who started a terrible pursuit. Vercassivellaunos in person was captured by the Romans as were 74 insignia. Sedullos, the leader of the Lemovices was killed. The defeat of the Gauls this time was complete. When he learned his cousin was routed, Vercingetorix called his troops still committed in the south back inside Alesia. Realising that all was lost, the relieving army soldiers still engaged on the rest of the front withdrew from the battlefield and took to their heels. At nightfall, now certain that his victory was complete, Caesar launched his cavalry in pursuit of the relief army but its rearguard was still well organised and drove off the Romans, causing them severe casualties. This was no longer of any importance since the knell for an independent Gaul had tolled once and for all at the very moment Vercassivellaunos had been routed and Vercingetorix had withdrawn back into Alesia.

VERCINGETORIX'S SURRENDER

The remains of the reinforcement army dissolved rapidly, fleeing towards each contingent's home territory. The only thing left for Vercingetorix to do now was surrender. He himself surrendered to Caesar the next day, recognising his failure. Caesar's account here is both sober, moving and very credible: *"the following day, Vercingetorix gathered the council together: he declared that he had not undertaken this war for personal gain but to re-conquer freedom for all; since he had to yield to fate, he offered himself to them and they could by their choice, appease the Romans with his death or hand him over alive to them. A deputation was sent to Caesar. He gave orders for all weapons*

to be handed over to him, and the leaders of the cities brought to him.

He set up his chair in the entrenchment, in front of his camp: it was there that the chiefs were brought to him; Vercingetorix was delivered to him, the weapons were thrown at his feet. He separated the prisoners, Aedui on one side and Arvernii on the other, thinking he would use these men to regain these people's confidence; and he distributed the others to the whole army as booty, one per head.” [18]

This was one quality that his enemies recognised: Caesar was a relatively magnanimous victor, for his epoch at least. He knew how to alternate acts of clemency - he let the warriors from the two biggest tribes in Gaul go free – with more pragmatic ones – he offered a prisoner as a slave to each of his legionaries – and symbolic mis en scenes, with the theatrical ceremony of Vercingetorix's surrender. Note, and this is often forgotten, that he also asked for the leaders of the rebel tribes to be handed over to him as hostages. With victory, the booty was enormous: one slave per Roman soldier; except for the Arvernii and the Aedui, this meant no fewer than 70 000 prisoners captured from among the besieged and the defeated in the relief army (mainly from the contingent led into the attack by Vercassivelaunos) who were offered, as a bonus with their pay, to the worthy soldiers in the Roman army. The soldiers usually sold their slave to merchants who followed the army to change this “present from Caesar” into cash.

During all the Gallic Wars, the estimate for the number of prisoners sold as slaves and dispatched to Italy or to other provinces amounted to almost a million. From an economic point of view, the massive influx of slave labour had decisive consequences on the development of the fading Republic's economy, breaking with its traditional structures. As for Vercingetorix, he finished his days in 46 BC in Rome. After six years spent in the darkest dungeons of the Tullianum prison, he was exhibited one last time for Caesar's triumph and then, now that he was of no use, strangled. The revolt's other chieftains probably, most of them, suffered a similar fate.

THE TRIUMPH OF ROMAN ORGANISA-TION

When he confronted the Roman army, unbeaten for more than fifty years throughout the whole Mediterranean area, did Vercingetorix really imagine he could win? The legions had methodically beaten the Gauls, first in Cisalpine Gaul then in the region of what was to become Transalpine Gaul. Did the last independent Gallic tribes really have any hope of escaping the Roman war machine?

In 52 BC, Vercingetorix, and particularly at Alesia, demonstrated that he had impressive political talent. He succeeded in mobilising and uniting a Gaul which was in decline and prey to internal divisions. He managed to make the most of the military qualities of the long-haired Gauls: forming a large army which he led to victory at Gergovia and on his own initiative mobilising a second even more formidable army to come and rescue him at Alesia. Politically effective, Vercingetorix was also a good military leader because he managed to immobilise the whole of Caesar's army for forty days. Defeating Caesar had been within his grasp several times, but the Roman muddling at Gergovia was not repeated. It was perhaps the pretence of victory at Gergovia which most influenced Vercingetorix's tactical choices at Alesia. Obviously the rebellion's leader tried to repeat the same type of battle at Alesia, assuming he would obtain the same results. But when Caesar chose not to make a direct attack on the Alesia oppidum, the rules changed.

By shutting himself up in his own system of earthworks, Caesar forced the Gauls to change from a tactical situation like that at the

Above.
German horsemen in Caesar's service.
(Illustration by H. de Nolhac, Private Collection)

Below.
The starving in front of the Alesia entrenchments.
(Illustration by H. de Nolhac, Private Collection)

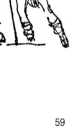

battle of Gergovia to that of attacking Roman camps, which to date had always failed. The way the Battle of Alesia unfolded in its final phase was a repetition of the model which had never been a great success for the Gauls: *"Mutatis mutandis, on a much bigger scale, there were there the principal features of the way the Gauls unsuccessfully attempted to capture Roman camps which had always ended with them sallying forth in strength."* [19] By deciding to join battle decisively at Alesia no doubt he took a well-advised decision in the light of his experience at Gergovia, but Caesar outdid him strategically. The proconsul in fact managed to reverse the direction of the fighting: Vercingetorix thought he could make Caesar attack Alesia but by blockading the oppidum with the circumvallation and the contravallation, Caesar finally forced the Gauls to attack his camps and their positions. From "defender" in a situation as favourable as it had been at Gergovia, Vercingetorix found himself in the role of "attacker "in a particularly dangerous context.

During the fighting itself, Caesar's genius lies in the fact that he reacted exactly as he had to at the critical moments, showing his keen powers of observation, his discernment and his personal involvement. Without direct contact with the relief army and its leaders (who were indeed in the same situation as he

was), Vercingetorix was unable to act in the same way to coordinate the Gallic forces and use his reserves. During the battles that took place around Alesia, the role of the cavalry was also a determining factor which might seem strange for a siege. Both the Gallic cavalry defeats at the foot of the oppidum, together with that which took place in the battle before they finally sought refuge inside Alesia, weighed heavily on the morale of the Gauls and on their freedom of movement. The action of Caesar's German mercenaries was decisive several times, notably at the end of the fighting between Vercassivellaunos and Labienus. By sacrificing the cavalry, their best soldiers, Vercingetorix then the chiefs of the relieving army without doubt compromised their opportunities. This cavalry would probably have been better used trying to obstruct the Roman army supplies instead of defying it in a series of pitched battles which were lost one after the other. In the end, although the qualities of Vercingetorix's soldiers cannot be denied – his effort was great and few chieftains had been able to push the Roman army into a corner as he had done – Caesar's worth as a general must remain better because he was an exception: *"Great war leaders in history are either meticulous and rigid men, attached to the manic respect of regulations in the camp and on the battlefield, or they are imaginative, unpredictable and original spirits. The former earn the respect but not the love of their men as long as they manage to prove that they are just as demanding with themselves as with their men, that their hardness is a rule of behaviour which has nothing fanciful about it and that they can be trusted under fire; The latter win the affection and the admiration of their troops by their unexpected reactions and their capacity for improvisation and initiative. Julius Caesar was in this second category and we might be allowed to think that these qualities were innate in him and had nothing to do with the manuals of military art (…) Even more importantly, Caesar knew how to lead by example (…) Caesar's actions all bear the hallmark of this suppleness, a quality which was a great succour to him in the trial which was the Civil War."* [20]

EPILOGUE

After his victory at Alesia, Caesar took his legions to winter in Aedui country. In 51 BC Caesar wound up his campaign by eliminating the last rebellious tribes. In the spring he marched into Bituriges territory, which he thoroughly devastated then he defeated the Carnutes.

Following page.
Vercingetorix's statue on top of the column, watching over the battlefield at Alesia. The original statue is in the grounds of the Chateau at Saint-Germain-en-Laye.
(Photograph: Private Collection, DR)

THAT YEAR'S BIG OPERATION was checking the vainglorious Bellovaci and their Belgian allies who had not wanted to join Vercingetorix so that they could have the distinction of defeating Caesar for themselves …Informed by his allies the Rhemi, Caesar nonetheless had to campaign for four months to crush these particular rebels. Then the proconsul sent troops to the Eburones and Labienus to the Treveri to finish off subjugating Northern Gaul before the end of the summer. In the west and centre-west, Caesar's two legates got the better of a certain Dumnacos, at the head of warriors from Aremorica and from the Liger (Loire) valley. The last great operation of 51 BC was the siege of Uxellodunum where two indomitable Gallic chiefs and their men had sought refuge: the Senones leader Drappes and the Cadurci chief Lucterios. Pursued then besieged by the legate Caninius, their stubborn resistance eventually obliged Caesar to go there himself. After a long siege, the oppidum only yielded in September after being deprived of water. Less magnanimous than was his wont, Caesar had all the hands of the captured Gauls hacked off as an example. He finished the year in Aquitania where the tribes submitted by themselves.

This time he dispersed his legions for the winter, four with the Belgians, two with the Aedui, two with the Turones and the last with the Lemovices (to watch over neighbouring Arvernii territory).

Below.
Very much inspired by the famous statue of the lying Gaul, the artist has shown Vercingetorix in his prison collapsing under the weight of Roman chains.
(Illustration by H. de Nolhac, Private Collection)

At the beginning of 50 BC, Caesar returned to Cisalpine Gaul where he was given a triumphal welcome, before returning to review his army which had at last beaten the Treveri. For the winter this time, he left two legions with the Treveri and four in Belgium. Two legions were recalled by the Senate. The war against the Gauls was over once and for all. Caesar returned to Cisalpine Gaul where only the XIIIth Legion was stationed.

The outcome of eight years of war was edifying: a few thousand Romans killed, about 700 000 Gauls massacred and from 500 000 to a million reduced to slavery. Christian Goudineau summarises this conflict appropriately by saying that "Caesar's campaigns stretched out over about 115 months. Caesar faced widespread opposition for only the three summer months of 52 BC. For 98% of the time his army was supported by auxiliaries from Transalpine Gaul and inner Gaul commanded by their own chieftains, supplied by the peoples of inner Gaul, and encountered the armed contingents and the civilian populations of other tribes in battle or besieged in their oppida. Sometimes a situation would cause a rift between one faction and another within a same people: brothers and parents fought against one another. Such a relatively small expeditionary corps would not have held out for such a long time without being helped by some form of collaboration."

The spark of Gallic resistance, lit by Vercingetorix at Alesia, continued to impress people despite the extent of Caesar's victory and its importance for Gaul, which then spent the next five centuries in Rome's protective and all-enveloping lap.

At first excluded from the founding myths of the Kings of France, who claimed they went back to the Franks, Vercingetorix "reappeared" in the 19th Century as a really national symbol. Napoleon III, then the IIIrd Republic, both venerated "our ancestors the Gauls" using Vercingetorix's struggle to unify Gaul as a model and to inspire the concept of "national defence" which later had a host of opportunities to illustrate itself, in 1870 and the two world wars. Today, when all that seems forgotten, the Battle of Alesia can assume its real significance, "beyond myth": that is, a battle among others and one of the last steps in the conquest of the "known" world by the Roman Republic. Alesia highlights both Caesar's exceptional military qualities and Vercingetorix's impressive authority. Indeed the latter had been able to keep an incredibly divided Gaul unified and also maintain the morale of its soldiers despite several setbacks. The nobility of the Gallic chieftain impressed as much the Ancients like Plutarch, as it did the Moderns.

The "drama" at Alesia cannot be forgotten because the struggle there was fierce and so significant for both Rome and Gaul.

"ALESIA, NO IDEA WHAT IT IS!"

These few pictures and topographical elements illustrate the site at Syam-Chaux des Crotenay (Department of Jura), which is the rival of the official site at Alise-Sainte-Reine as the site of the siege of Alesia.

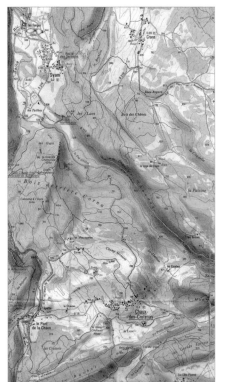

Opposite and below.
Map and satellite view of the site at Syam and the various fortified Gallic and Roman elements. View of the plain. The Syam site.

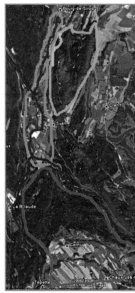

The Syam site, an illustration from the 19th Century. In the background the oppidum. *(Private Collection, DR)*

The citadel seen from the plain, at the Syam site.

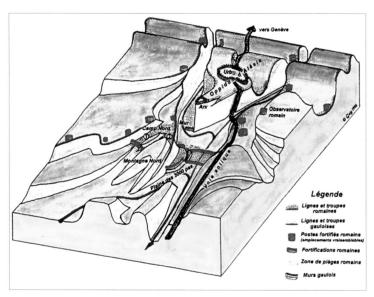

Cut-away of the Syam site. *(Private Collection, DR)*

(Private Collection, RR)

Bibliography

CLASSICAL SOURCES
— Caesar, The War of the Gauls
— Diodorus of Sicily, Historical Library
— Dion Cassius, Roman History
— Florus, Tableau
— Orosius, History against the Pagans
— Plutarch, Life of Caesar
— Strabo, Geographia
— Suetonius, the Lives of the Twelve Caesars
— Tacitus, Annal
— Titus Livius, Roman History
— Velleius Paterculus, Roman History

ABOUT ALÉSIA
— André Berthier and André Wartelle, Alésia
 (Nouvelles Editions Latines 1990)
— Antoinette Brenet, Les escargots de la Muluccha (Institut Vitruve 1996)
— Jérôme Carcopino, Alésia et les ruses de César (Flammarion 1970)
— Peter Inker, Caesar's Gallic Triumph : The battle of Alesia 52 BC
 (Pen & Sword Military 2008)
— Joël Le Gall, Alésia (Fayard 1963)
— Michel Reddé, Alésia, l'archéologie face à l'imaginaire
 (Editions Errance 2003)

ABOUT THE GALLIC WARS
— Christian Goudineau, César et la Gaule (Editions Errance 1997)
— José Ignacio Lago, Las campañas de Julio César (Almeida 2004)
— Philippe Richardot, Les erreurs stratégiques des Gaulois face à César
 (Economica 2006)
— Philippe Richardot, César et sa stratégie de conquête des Gaules
 (dans les magazines Prétorien n°7 et n°8 2008)

ABOUT CAESAR AND VERCINGETORIX
— Luca Canali, De Jules César à Jésus-Christ (Arléa 2006)
— Jérôme Carcopino, Profils de conquérants (Flammarion 1992)
— Jacques Harmand, Vercingétorix (Fayard 1994)
— Eberhart Horst, César (Fayard 1981)
— Yann Le Bohec, César chef de guerre (Editions du Rocher 2001)
— Jean Markale, Vercingétorix (Hachette 1982)
— Zvi Yaretz, César et son image (Les Belles Lettres 1990)

ABOUT ROMAN AND GALLIC ARMIES
— Peter Connolly, Greece and Rome at War (Greenhill Books 1998)
— Hans Delbrück, History of Art of War, Volume I (Bison Books 1990)
— Michel Feugère, Les armes des Romains (Editions Errance 1993)

— Stephan Fichtl, La ville celtique, les oppida (Editions Errance 2005)
— Franck Mathieu, Le guerrier gaulois (Editions Errance 2007)
— Jane Penrose, Rome and Her Enemies (Osprey Publishing 2005)
— Michel Reddé (sous la direction de), L'armée romaine en Gaule
 (Editions Errance 1996)

HISTORY GAMES
— G. Weber, Alésia (Jeux Descartes 1985)
— Richard H. Berg and Mark Herman, Alesia (GMT Games 2005)
— Frédéric Bey and Marc Brandsma, Bellum Gallicum
 (Casus Belli n°68 et n°69 1992)
— Frédéric Bey, Alésia, 52 avant J.-C. (Vae Victis n°21 1998)
— Frédéric Bey, Alésia, l'hypothèse jurassienne (Canons en Carton 2005)

Author's note

The present book has used the sources which are available today and does not incorporate current archaeological and palaeographical research or even discoveries which could be revealed in the future. The French translation of the Bellum Gallicum used as a reference in spite of some uncertainties is that by L.-A. Constans (Les Belles Lettres).

FOOT NOTES
1. Christian Goudineau: César et les Gaules (Caesar and the Gauls).
2. Jacques Harmand, Vercingétorix
3. Luca Canali: De Jules César à Jésus-Christ (from Julius Caesar to Jesus Christ)
4. Suetonius: The Lives of the Twelve Caesars
5. Luca Canali: De Jules César à Jésus Christ
6. Christian Goudineau: César et la Gaule (Caesar and Gaul)
7. Philippe Richardot: César et sa stratégie de conquête des Gaules (Caesar and his strategy conquering the Gauls)
8. Caesar: Bellum Gallicum, Book I.40
9. Caesar: Bellum Gallicum, Book I.
110. Art de conduire un siège
11. An army's baggage and supply train, slowing down its advance.
12. Caesar: Bellum Gallicum, Book VII.69
13. Caesar: Bellum Gallicum, Book VII.70
14. Antoinette Brenet: Vae Victis N°20
15. Caesar: Bellum Gallicum, Book VII, 75
16. Caesar: Bellum Gallicum, Book VII, 81
17. Caesar: Bellum Gallicum, Book VII, 87
18. Caesar: Bellum Gallicum, Book VII, 89
19. Christian Goudineau: César et la Gaule (Caesar and Gaul)
20. Zvi Yavetgz: César et son image (Caesar and his image)
21. Christian Goudineau: César et la Gaule

Thanks

The author would like to thank Jacques Motreff and Olivier Velin for their shrewd advice,
Patrick Boos of the *"les Gaulois de l'Esse"* Society and Patrick Berbérian of the *"Limitis"* Society,
as well as Serge Baudouard for the quality of his illustrations.

Conception & layout: Jean-Marie Mongin
© *Histoire & Collections 2011*

Cover. Oil by Henri Motte, Giraudon, Musée Crozatier, le Puy-en-Velay. Inset. Illustration by S. Baudouard. Maps after the works of Ludovic Moignet and Yann Kervran

A book published by
HISTOIRE & COLLECTIONS
SA au capital de 182 938,82 €
5, avenue de la République
F-75541 Paris Cedex 11 FRANCE
Tél. 33 1 40 21 18 20 - Fax 33 1 47 00 51 11
www.histoireetcollections.fr

This book has been designed,
typed, laid-out and processed
by *Histoire & Collections,*
fully on integrated computer equipment

Print run completed
in June 2011
on the presses of Zure,
Spain, European Union